Strategic Planning, Systems Analysis, and Database Design

Strategic Planning, Systems Analysis, and Database Design

The Continuous Flow Approach

Mark L. Gillenson
IBM Systems Research Institute

Robert Goldberg
IBM Software Engineering Institute

A Wiley-Interscience Publication

John Wiley & Sons

New York / Chichester / Brisbane / Toronto / Singapore

Library of Congress Cataloging in Publication Data:
Gillenson, Mark L.
    Strategic planning, systems analysis, and database
design.

    "A Wiley-Interscience publication."
    Includes indexes
    1. Corporate planning—Data processing. 2. System
analysis—Data processing. I. Goldberg, Robert.
II. Title.
HD30.28.G54   1983   658.4'012'02854   83-10212
ISBN 0-471-89066-9

Printed in the United States of America

10 9 8 7 6 5 4 3 2 1

To Barbara

To Toba

Preface

Computers have become an ever-present part of the way in which we do business today, so commonplace that we often forget that they are relative newcomers in the management of organizations. At the same time though, their use has been shrouded in a mystique that has prevented their becoming integrated into the way we control our organizations. It is the claim of this book that the time is past when we have the luxury of considering business planning and the use of computers as separate little cubicles that need never consult each other.

The discipline of planning has grown over the last several years and is becoming a commonplace tool for executives. The phrases used to describe data processing are becoming accepted by these same executives. At the same time, several disciplines have grown in the technical fields of data processing that can control it and mold it to become more predictable and manageable. These latter fall into the province of systems analysis and database design.

Databases and the information they contain are recognized by most as a great step forward in the controlling of organizations. Data as a resource is moving from the pens of the theoreticians into the recommendations of the consultants and finally into the accepted world of the executive. Such ideas and techniques need to be merged with those of organizational planning.

At the same time, the software engineers are creating many techniques that will change the development of useful applications into a dependable trade. Applications are the stuff from which plans are made, and executives and planners need to be able to understand the terms of this specialty.

The combination of these three areas: strategic planning, systems analysis, and database design, represents a potential that has only been realized in a limited number of locations. Is there some uniform set of steps that an organization should use to merge these areas? Do the techniques chosen depend on some aspect of the organization? Is there some continuous flow of techniques that ought to be used to ease the pain of development? These are the questions this book was written to address. The book is designed for professionals working in either of these three fields who require a roadmap through the approaches of the other disciplines. It is written at a tutorial level and as such will also be applicable as a senior business school course or as a part of an MBA curriculum.

The authors of this book owe a debt of gratitude to the management of the IBM Systems Research Institute for its encouragement in endeavors such as this book. The climate engendered by Erich Bloch, IBM Vice President, Technical Personnel Development enabled us to complete this work.

We thank R.W. DeSio, the director of the IBM Systems Research Institute, and our respective managers at various times, Mr. Roy E. Heistand, Mr. John H. Morrissey, and Mr. Allen L. Morton, Jr. for all those things that a manager must do to provide the opportunity for an undertaking of this nature to be brought to successful completion.

We also wish to thank Ms. Judy King who read and commented on several chapters, providing advice that strengthened the book.

Finally, we would like to thank our colleagues at the IBM Systems Research Institute and throughout IBM, for all the discussions that create the intellectual atmosphere which makes a book possible.

MARK L. GILLENSON
ROBERT GOLDBERG

New York, New York
November 1983

Contents

Contents

SECTION I

The Working Environment

1

Introduction

THE NEED FOR PLANNING AND CONTROL

Organizations exist to achieve a goal. Whether the organization is an industrial concern that manufactures goods for a profit, or a beehive whose residents instinctively cooperate for survival, there is some reason for the organization's existence.

Human organizations, profit-making or otherwise, can be dissected in several different ways for further study. For example, an organization can be viewed as a hierarchy of people, with different branches of the hierarchy having different and far-ranging responsibilities. It can be viewed as a system that takes in inputs from the outside world, processes them, and generates outputs in response. An organization can be considered to be a system that, given proper management and the availability of resources, can ultimately produce some desired goal.

Regardless of how one chooses to characterize an organization, it is clear that the various components must be managed effectively. There must be a fundamental sense of understanding of how a component functions. There must be a way to measure its performance. There must be a set of plans for its future development, in concert with the plans for all of the other components. There must be mechanisms for reaction to unforeseen occurrences.

Modern organizations have come to rely increasingly on the computer both as an operational tool and as a management tool. The material that enables the computer to be an effective tool is data: data that describes the organizational components, and mirrors the flow of goods and services—from employee profiles, to customer invoices, to sales records, ranging through all aspects of a business. An organization's data may not only be used for day-to-day management, but may also be used for tactical and strategic planning. In fact, data is the first and foremost corporate resource because without data on other resources, there can be no effective control.

DATA AND COMPUTERS

The Origins of Record Keeping

Mankind has been interested in data for at least the last 12,000 years. While today we often associate the concept of data with the computer, there have, historically, been many, more primitive methods of data handling, some of which are still in use today.

In present-day Iraq, one can find shepherds who keep track of their flocks with pebbles. As each sheep leaves its pen to graze, the shepherd places one pebble in a small sack. When the sheep return, the shepherd discards one pebble for each animal, and thus has a way of knowing whether he has lost any of his flock. This method of record keeping is a variation of the most ancient method known.

Excavations in the Zagros region of Iran, dated 8500 BC, have unearthed clay tokens or "counters" which, it is theorized, were used for record keeping. Such tokens have been found in sites from present-day Turkey to Pakistan and as far afield as Khartoum. They date from as long ago as 7000 BC.

By 3000 BC, at present-day Susa in Iran, the use of such tokens had reached a greater level of sophistication. Tokens, with special markings on them, were sealed in hollow clay vessels, which apparently represented bills of lading, accompanying commercial goods in transit. The tokens represented the quantity of goods being shipped and, obviously, could not be tampered with without the clay vessels being broken open. Inscriptions on the outside of the vessels, and the seals of the parties involved, provided a further record. The external inscriptions included words or concepts such as *deposited, transferred,* and *removed.*

At about the same time that the Susa culture existed, people in a city-state in Sumeria called Uruk kept records in clay texts. With pictographs, numerals, and ideographs, they described land sales and business transactions involving bread, beer, sheep, cattle, and clothing.

Other neolithic means of record-keeping included storing tallies as cuts and notches on wooden sticks and as knots in rope. The former procedure continued in use in England as late as the medieval period; the latter was used by South American Indians.

Data Through the Ages

In retrospect, the primary original interest in data can be traced to the rise of cities. Simple, subsistence hunting, gathering, and, later, agrarian cultures had little use for the concept of data. But, as we have seen with Susa and Uruk, cities and the attendant culture that began with the Bronze Age forever changed the way mankind lived. The beginnings of mass production, the specialization of labor, the use of money, and the bartering of services and products for the necessities of life, all required the keeping of data in records.

As time went on, more and different kinds of data and records were kept, including calendars, census data, surveys, land ownership records, marriage records, data on temple contributions, and family trees. Merchants had to keep track of inventories, shipments, and wage payments, in addition to production itself. As farming went beyond the subsistence level and entered the feudal and succeeding stages, there was a need to keep data on the amount of produce to consume, to barter with, and to retain as seed for the following year.

The participation of Europeans in the Crusades, which took place from the late eleventh to the late thirteenth centuries, created as a side effect a broader view of the world and a correspondingly greater interest in trade. A common method of trade during that era was the establishment of partnerships among merchants, ships captains, and owners to facilitate commercial voyages. This increased level of commercial sophistication brought with it another round of increasingly complex record-keeping, specifically, double-entry bookkeeping.

Double-entry bookkeeping originated in the trading centers of fourteenth-century Italy. The earliest-known example is from a merchant in Genoa and dates to the year 1340. Its use gradually spread, but it was not until 1494 in Venice (about 25 years after the first movable-type printing press in Venice came into use), that a Franciscan Monk named Luca Pacioli published his *Summa de Arithmetica, Geometrica, Proportioni et Proportionalita*, a work that had the important effect of spreading the use of double-entry bookkeeping. Of course, the increasing use of paper and the printing press, additional contributing factors, furthered the advance of record-keeping at that time as well.

As the dominance of the Italian merchants declined, other countries became more active traders, and, concomitantly, users of data and keepers of records. Furthermore, as the use of temporary trading partnerships declined, and more stable, long-term mercantile organizations were established, other types of data became necessary. For example, annual, as opposed to venture-by-venture, statements of profit and loss were needed. In 1673 the *Code of Commerce* in France required that a balance sheet be drawn up every two years by every businessman.

Early Calculating Devices

It was also in the seventeenth century that people began to take an interest in devices that could "automatically" process data, if only in a rudimentary way. One of the earliest and best-known such creations was produced by Blaise Pascal, in France in the 1640s, reportedly to help his father do his job as a tax commissioner. It was a small box containing interlocking gears capable of doing addition and subtraction. In fact, it was the forerunner of today's automobile odometers.

In about 1694, Gottfried Wilhelm von Leibniz built a more sophisticated device, consisting of cylinders and wheels with interlocking teeth. It was capable of multiplying and dividing, with one multidigit number entered initially, and the other represented by turning a gear that number of times. Like Pascal's, Leibniz's device suffered, in practical use, from the poor machining skills of the day, but its principles were to be used in fairly contemporary mechanical calculating devices.

In France in 1805, Joseph Marie Jacquard invented a device that automatically created patterns during the textile weaving process. The heart of the device was a series of cards with holes punched in them; the holes allowed strands of material to be interwoven in a sequence that produced the desired pattern. While Jacquard's loom was not a calculating device as such, his method of storing fabric patterns as holes in punched cards was a very clever means of data storage, which would have great importance for later computing devices.

The last of the early computing geniuses was truly a man ahead of his time. Charles Babbage was a nineteenth-century English mathematician. During the 1820s and 1830s he developed and built a machine that he called the "Difference Engine." Sophisticated for its time, it was capable of tabulating series of numbers derived from complicated polynomials. Such tables were needed in navigation and astronomy. Beginning in 1833, Babbage began to think about another invention which he called the "Analytical Engine." He never completed it (again, the state of the machinist's art lagged behind the creativity of the mind), but included in its design were many of the principles of modern computers. The Analytical Engine was to consist of a "store" for holding data items and a "mill" for operating upon them. Babbage was very impressed by Jacquard's work with punched cards. In fact, the Analytical Engine was to be able to store calculation instructions in punched cards, which would be fed into the machine together with punched cards containing data to operate on that data and produce the desired result.

Practical Large-Scale Calculating

The development of practical computing and tabulating devices required two things: a large-scale data storage and processing capability and a certain basic level of manufacturing skills to produce adequate mechanical and electrical devices. By the late nineteenth century, machining skills, which had reached a sufficiently advanced level, were called upon to meet a pressing informational need: the compilation of the U.S. Census.

The 1880 U.S. Census took about seven years to compile by hand. It was estimated that using the same, manual techniques, the compilation of the 1890 census would not be completed until after the 1900 census data had begun to be collected. The solution was provided by a government engineer named Herman Hollerith. Basing this work on Jacquard's punched card concept (as had Babbage), he built devices to punch holes in cards and devices to sort them. Wire brushes touching the cards completed circuits when they came across the holes, and thereby advanced electromechanical counters. Using Hollerith's equipment, the total population count of the 1890 census was completed one month after all of the data was in. The complete set of tabulations, including data on questions that had never before been practical to ask, took two years. In 1896, Hollerith formed the Tabulating Machine Company to produce and commercially market his devices. That company, combined with several others, eventually formed what is today the International Business Machines Corporation (IBM).

The Census Bureau, while using Hollerith's equipment, continued experimenting on its own. One of its engineers, James Powers, developed devices to automatically feed cards into the equipment and to automatically print results. In 1911 he formed the Powers Tabulating Machine Company, which eventually formed the basis for the Univac division of the Sperry Rand Corporation.

During the 1920s and 1930s, Vannevar Bush at the Massachusetts Institute of Technology and others at such institutions as the Moore

School of Engineering of the University of Pennsylvania developed important "analog" computers (based on continuous measuring devices, in contrast to those that counted discrete items, such as holes in cards), primarily for military ballistics calculations.

As World War II approached, the pace of development quickened. George R. Stibitz at Bell Labs and Howard H. Aiken at Harvard produced sophisticated electromechanical, digital computers. Aiken's Mark I, completed in 1944, had 72 numerical "counters," or storage positions, and took five seconds to do a multiplication operation.

The first large, viable, fully electronic computer was also hastened by the ballistics needs of the military during the war. Called the ENIAC (Electronic Numerical Integrator and Computer) it was begun in 1943 at the Moore School by John W. Mauchly and J. Presper Eckert, and was completed in 1946. It had 18,000 vacuum tubes and could perform 5,000 additions per second. It was about 1,000 times faster than the Mark I.

With the advance into fully electronic computers having been made, other developments followed rapidly. In 1945, John von Neumann proposed a stored-program computer. The first such machine, called the EDSAC, was completed at Cambridge University in England in 1949 by Maurice Wilkes. The first machine with core memory was the MIT Whirlwind I, also of the late 1940s.

Commercial Computers

In 1947, Eckert and Mauchly formed a company, and in 1951 delivered the UNIVAC I (Universal Automatic Computer) to the census bureau. That company was eventually absorbed by Remington Rand (later Sperry Rand), which continued to produce computers with the UNIVAC name. IBM, which had a very strong presence with electromechanical calculating equipment and some early vacuum tube-based devices, produced its first electronic computer in 1953. The IBM 701 was a scientifically oriented machine with a vacuum tube memory. It was followed by the business-oriented 702 and then in 1955 by the 705, which had a core memory. Those machines, and others like them, came to be known as "first-generation" computers.

The late 1950s and early 1960s saw the advent of transistor-, as op-

posed to vacuum tube-based computers. These machines, which became
the "second-generation" computers, were much more reliable, smaller,
and faster than those of the first generation. In addition to being incorporated into large computers, this new technology, combined with
improvements in core memory technology, created the first viable
smaller-scale computers, which became highly successful and prolifer-
ated at a rapid rate. Such machines were the first computers for many
thousands of corporations.

The mid- and late 1960s saw the rise of the "third generation" of
computers. Based on integrated circuits, third-generation computers
were another major step forward. They also incorporated increasingly
sophisticated input and output devices and secondary storage devices,
particularly moving-head disk units.

Today's Data Processing Environment

Eventually, the boundaries between computer generations became in-
distinct. We speak of today's fourth generation of computers as being
based on "very large scale integrated" (VLSI) circuits. That technology
and countless other improvements have continued the simultaneous
trend of decreasing price and increasing performance.

Computers now range from desktop "home" or "micro" computers,
to incredibly powerful large machines. Storage facilities have become
faster, more reliable, and capable of packing data in an increasingly
dense fashion. Networks of far-flung computers, tied together by a
variety of communications media, have flourished.

Software, the various kinds of instructions that make the machines
run, has also continuously advanced. Highly sophisticated operating
systems allow many people to use the machines simultaneously. Database management systems permit nonredundant data storage and complex data access. Special development systems permit certain application
programs to be quickly created, subverting the slow, traditional programming process.

In short, the computer has progressed to the point where it can
become a part of virtually every business process, a trend that is sure
to continue.

STRATEGIC PLANNING, SYSTEMS ANALYSIS, AND DATABASE DESIGN

The Four Stages of Planning and Design

Computers today play a key role in the management of virtually every kind of profit-making and nonprofit organization. The data that is gathered, stored, and used by these concerns has come to be recognized as a legitimate and very important organizational resource. That being the case, the management of and the planning for the computer and its related data resources—the information systems environment—must be an integral part of management's plans for the organization as a whole.

In this book we will discuss four major phases of planning that involve an organization's information systems environment.

The first phase is *business strategic planning*. To make plans for an organization's information systems resource, there must be a well-developed plan for the growth of the overall organization.

The second phase is *information systems strategic planning*. Given the business strategic plan, planning can and must be done for the development of the information systems that must grow to meet the ever-increasing size and expectations of the rest of the firm. Planning at this stage is still high level in nature.

The third phase is *detailed systems analysis*. To carry the information systems strategic plan to fruition, a detailed study must be made of each business process, so that the computer as a tool can be effectively integrated into business operations.

Finally, in the fourth phase, the data identified by the detailed systems analysis must be developed further for the specific computer system to be used. This work is called *database design*.

The Book's Organization

The book is organized into three sections: *the business environment, the phases of information systems planning and data design,* and *the integrated, continuous-flow approach.*

The first section, the business environment, looks at the pressures acting on today's management—from the general environment, with its increased pace of change, and from issues related to modern data processing, such as the centralization or decentralization of resources.

In the second section of the book we discuss the four phases of planning, relative to information systems. After further definition, we will give additional details about each phase, including a discussion of the various processes and techniques that have been developed by which each phase is completed.

In the third section we examine the threads that link each of the phases together and discuss their implications for the future.

The plan of the book can be imagined to follow the path of a spiral in which each section comes around one more time, expanding in size and scope, showing the transitions that occur as we travel from strategic planning to systems analysis to database design. Each of the sections will follow a pattern of describing the problem and elucidating and expanding on the ways shown to have worked in approaching a solution to the problem. In this manner each of the three sections will visit similar areas, but with a point of view that has expanded to include more detail.

BIBLIOGRAPHY

Gleiser, M., "Men and Machines Before Babbage," *DATAMATION,* vol. 24, no. 10, October 1978, pp. 125–130.

Goldstine, H. H., *The Computer from Pascal to von Neumann,* Princeton University Press, Princeton, NJ, 1972.

Gordon, M. J., and Shillinglaw, G., *Accounting: A Management Approach,* 4th ed., Richard D. Irwin, Homewood, IL, 1969.

Henriksen, E. S., *Accounting Theory,* rev. ed., Richard D. Irwin, Homewood, IL, 1970.

Littleton, A. C., and Yamey, B. S., *Studies in the History of Accounting,* Richard D. Irwin, Homewood, IL, 1956.

Rosen, S., "Electronic Computers: A Historical Survey," *Computing Surveys,* vol. 1, no. 1, March 1969, pp. 7–36.

Schmandt-Besserat, D., "The Earliest Precursor of Writing," *Scientific American,* vol. 238, no. 6, June 1978, pp. 50–59.

Tropp, H., "The Effervescent Years: A Retrospective," *IEEE Spectrum,* vol. 11, no. 2, February 1974, pp. 70–79.

2

The Business Environment

THE COMPUTER AS A BUSINESS TOOL

An Operational Tool

Businesses and other organizations, always subject to many pressures, continually face demands for more efficient use of resources and for a more "rational" decision-making process. Computers, with their capacity for keeping track of small details, have become one of the means with which these results can be achieved.

The analogy that comes to mind is a thermostat, which controls the temperature of the environment. Only by being constantly aware of the temperature and the direction in which it is changing are we able to effectively control that aspect of our environment. Computers perform an analogous function for an increasingly wide variety of organizational functions. Daily operations are monitored to a degree not dreamed of several decades ago. Organizations can use resources that would otherwise be idle. The responses that are possible have been drawn down to the daily and even hourly cycles of the business and have entered the domain of the operational managers.

An Informational Tool

The use of computers to improve the daily, operational level of an organization only begins to identify their power. Although portions of organizations can be thought of as well-oiled machines that can be controlled by keeping track of their resources, other segments are more like "knowledge factories" in which a slight edge in the timeliness of information or its availability at a particular place is the key ingredient of success.

The structure of businesses is beginning to change because of the new information era. The functions and organizations that have evolved over the last century are being refined by information availability. Some definitions and structures will remain, and others will be replaced by more efficient forms. In the next section we will begin to look at some current definitions and begin the evolutionary process toward computer-described functions and tasks.

BUSINESS DESCRIPTION

Businesses (and not-for-profit organizations) do not exist without a purpose. They have objectives to meet to survive. Some try merely to survive, where others try to expand their horizons and provide goods and services to a growing customer set. In today's complex environment, no single individual is capable of managing all aspects of a business. To satisfy its survival and management requirements, a business organizes.

BUSINESS ORGANIZATION

Organizational structure has evolved over the last century into its current form so that the goals and objectives of the owners/managers can be better met. As the complexity of management outran the general abilities of entrepreneurs and founders, problems were solved by specialists and through the delegation of authority. The original structures were assembled to achieve particular managerial ends, and while some of the attempts succeeded extremely well, others failed. What we are left with today is the residue of that delegation of authority that occurred to make organizations manageable.

Levels of Management

The delegation of authority from entrepreneurs to managers eventually stabilized into patterns of control and decision making for which generic definitions of task could be made. Hierarchic levels identified the range and span of organizational control that was delegated to the individuals who filled the managerial slots. The levels were eventually called *general management, functional management,* and *operational management.* An alternate set of names is top, middle, and operational management.[1]

The theory of organizational structure identifies patterns and flows of information, control, and decision making. Control, it is said, flows from the top to the bottom, while information, in response to control, flows from the bottom to the top. Decisions are made at the proper level to support the related flows of control and information. Computational capability within the organization should then be set to support the flows of information and control if it is to serve the organization effectively. This implies that the placement of systems and equipment and the control of these items must serve total organizational goals as well as individual goals.

Levels of Decision Making

Strategic. Decision making at the strategic level is done very broadly. The managers who occupy this level try to set broad organizational directives and establish priorities. It is not the job of strategic planners to operationally administer a set of goals; it is their job to identify the direction to be followed.

Tactical. Tactical decision makers receive the objectives of the strategic planners and begin to assemble the resources required. If a decision needs to be made about the allocation of resources, the tactical planners will decide priorities among competing needs. The major task at this level is to identify the plans and resources required to carry out the strategic objectives that have been decided upon by the strategic decision makers. The time horizon at the tactical decision level is measured in months, whereas the horizon of the strategic decision makers is measured in five to ten year increments.

Operational. Operational control attempts to bring about the tasks selected at the strategic level. The employees at this level are concerned with carrying out a specific function. This group sets in motion and decides directly about concrete activity. Its time horizon is thus tomorrow.

APPLICATION TYPES

Why Differences Between Types Are Crucial

The support given an organization by its data processing function comes in the form of the automation of business processes. The set of computer programs that embodies the automated business process is a computer application. In expert discussions of applications, there has been a tendency to focus attention on the process of producing the system rather than on the application itself. We describe the application development process or the application development problem. This approach lumps all the programs written in a computer center together and tries—unsuccessfully—the same techniques to improve them in common. If an attempt is made to classify applications according to any number of criteria, it becomes clear that there exist separate and distinct classes of applications that require different prescriptions and approaches if they are to be created and maintained effectively.

The applications that have evolved fall within the following general categories: *operational control systems, informational systems, decision systems,* and *tools systems.* Each of these has its own set of characteristics and demands its own environment. The four categories deliberately exclude "systems" programs, which are so different that one cannot discuss them in the same context as application programs.

Operational Control Systems

The programs that support the operational control level of the organization are involved in the daily operations of the business. While it is true that any organization that does not plan will have a difficult time when the future arrives, it is also true that any organization that does not transact its daily business well will not survive long enough for it to matter how well it has predicted the future. Survival is the first requirement and requires good operational control programs. These are the programs usually thought of as *the computer programs* of the organization.

Transaction-Driven. Transaction-driven programs are designed to handle the routine paperwork that has traditionally been done manually. Many discrete transactions, upon entering a department, are responded to one at a time by the department personnel. Each of these transactions must be processed in detail, and although there are slight discrepancies between each order, invoice, phone call, and so forth, each follows a particular pattern prescribed for that transaction. Because a transaction represents a single, reasonably specialized task, the programming to automate it is simple. The difficulties in operational control systems tend to involve the high data volumes, the storage requirements that are characteristic of them, and the efficiency of the computation process.

Process-Oriented. The arrival of computers allows us to think of reintegrating some of the functions that had been separated because of the evolved need to delegate authority. Once again we are returning to a way of doing business in which we can think about all of the aspects of a transaction. An example might be airlines reservations in which an initial, limited application has had its scope continually increased so that all the ramifications of a particular reservation can be taken into account at the same time. Today the airlines reservation clerk reserves seats and meals, orders special meals, arranges for connecting flights, and so on. This broad scope of activity forces us to concentrate on the processes of the business (more on this subject later).

Triggered. The structure of the operational control programs thus becomes clear. A set of transactions enter the organization, trigger consequences in other departments or locations until the trail of cause and effect leaves the organization behind. The set of functions and tasks joined by these transactions and their relationships then represents the organizational process that is managed.

The computer is an ideal tool for connecting the elements of an organization's work flow, even when the connecting links are organizationally or geographically remote from each other.

Current-Time Horizon. Operational control programs are required on the spot by the manager for today's work. This means that part of the manager's job directly involves using or feeding a computer. When a problem occurs the manager who is affected is the first-line manager. If we compare the operations of a petrochemical complex, driven by computers that control each process in an attempt to achieve optimal results, to the effect of the operational control applications, then these applications represent the process control of the organization.

Nondeferrable. Operational applications are the bread and butter of the organization. Tied to its survival, they consequently must run according to their fixed schedules, or the organization will show a real loss of resources. The consequence is that all the operational features of a data center are tied together as in a single knot. If the system must run on time, and the data volumes that are processed increase, then the amount of time required to process each day's lot will also increase. Similarly, experience teaches us that the more successful a system is, the more people want to use it and the more they want to add to it. This tendency has the same effect on capacity. We are continually running out of processing capacity. For these programs, efficiency is the key to processing the workload with the given computer resources in the required time.

Informational Systems

Informational programs, as the name implies, provide answers to questions. These questions are asked by functional or middle management during the course of their work. Operational control systems do provide information, but on a regular and very inflexible basis. Informational programs on the other hand are those that help provide answers to questions that are out of the ordinary.

Informational programs generally respond to particular outside factors tracked in the computer. The data bases already exist and are being monitored in some continuous fashion. Managers, noticing deviations from planned occurrences, respond by looking at specific combinations of already existing data. The processing content of the manager's view is low. Thus in this environment the goal is to provide answers to ad hoc questions on as efficient a basis as possible.

Extractive. Most of the information accumulated by the operational control systems is available to answer unanticipated questions. If a manager notices an exception to a planned or expected course of events, the data managed by the operational control systems are reviewed and queried, and a report is extracted that contains the information requested.

Future-Time Horizon. When an informational program is run, the output is used to help a decision maker choose a future course of action. Delays of one hour in answering such inquiries would be less important than a similar delay in an operational control system.

Deferrable. The reports thus produced tend to be less urgent. For example, compare the output of the payroll program to the output of the program run to check variances in levels of inventory. Yes, the inventory is important, but if the employees are not paid and stop working, the inventory levels will no longer be important. In this instance, every one of us would accept the deferral of the inventory report in favor of running the checks.

Limited Lifetime. Those programs known as informational systems tend to vary one from the other. Just as predicting the future is a risky business, so too is specifying a program that supplies information to be used to help make future decisions. These programs will be volatile and of limited life. In particular studies show that most programs in this category tend to survive for less than six months, and have development costs that far exceed the cost of operating them in their total lifetimes.

For these programs, the key is flexibility. Managers who require this information understand that their perception of what is required changes as their experience grows. For the program to be a viable tool the turn-around time of development becomes crucial; hence the limiting constraint for informational programs is the speed at which the programming community can provide programs.

Tool Systems

Operational control and informational systems represent the organizationally mandated use of computers. The information stored by operational control systems is maintained in a particular format specified by the standards of the organization. Use of this data requires that these standards and formats be strictly adhered to. There is little freedom of choice available to the one who must use this data. Computers, however, have uses that are not constrained and that allow a great deal of flexibility. Certain computer programs are general-purpose tools that assist employees in solving a particular problem. For example someone doing forecasting may discover a particularly well-suited statistical package that makes the analysis much simpler. These programs represent tools that one can use to get one's job done. Decision makers choose them, buy them, and often even jealously guard them.

Interchangeable. Interchangeability is the distinguishing attribute of a tool. When one needs to deliver a response, and the method of arriving at that response is unimportant, then that method represents a tool. An engineer, for example, who does a calculation may use a pencil and paper, a slide rule, a hand-held calculator, a small personal computer, or a large computer. If the result is accurate, the choice of mechanism does not matter. Which mechanism is used is a matter of personal preference and convenience. The tool that is chosen is usually capable of being personalized to a particular individual style. This implies some lack of general use since a personalized program need not be acceptable to someone else, even if they are doing exactly the same function. Tools tend to enter organizations in secret, bloom, mature, and become irreplaceable.

Decision Support Systems

Decision support systems represent one kind of tool that a manager may require. They are related to the types already described and may share the characteristics of several. They represent a particular use of computers by individuals to augment human capabilities with controllable machine characteristics. Decision support systems tend to be concerned with "beating" nature. The intent is to arrive at a decision that maximizes business performance. The processing content of this type of environment is usually high. The decision maker creates models that try to predict the future. For this environment the key design attribute is user satisfaction. When the user is technically oriented, then the result may appear incomprehensible to any other similarly trained employee. When, on the other hand, the decision maker is not knowledgeable about computers, the result must be easy to use. A decision support system must be freely chosen by its user, or it will not be used effectively.

INCREASING CONTROL BY COMPUTER

The computer resources of an organization serve at least three masters. The first is the user, the direct beneficiary of the computer's services and the one whom most discussions focus around. The data processing professionals require an expanding resource and have a vested interest in providing applications. The third group is the management of the organization, which uses the information produced by the computer to control the organization better.

The Role of Standards

Control of an organization is achieved by making certain that the vocabulary used by the individual components is widely understood, not only by the individual managers, but also in a forced way, if necessary, by peers. The standards organizations are the vehicle to ensure the existence of a common vocabulary. Their function is rarely understood by any of the three groups to whom computer resources are dedicated.

Auditing Requirements

An example of where this standards function applies is in providing systems analysis and operational control of software which enhances the auditability of the function. Increased auditability is rarely the primary concern of the direct user of the software. Difficult to do consistently, auditability is rarely high on data processing's list. The only group that must push for auditability is management, which needs accurate information for control and reporting purposes.

The foregoing categorization of software leads to the conclusion that the goals of management will be supported differently in each of the application types described above. A sensitivity to these distinctions is important if one is to understand where and how data processing resources ought to be applied within an organization.

REFERENCES

1. Murdick, R. G. and Ross, J. E., *Information Systems for Modern Management*, 2d ed., Prentice-Hall, Englewood Cliffs, NJ, 1975.

QUESTIONS FOR THOUGHT

1. Choose a functional area of a corporation, such as finance, manufacturing, etc. Compile a list of some of the major strategic, tactical, and operational decisions that must be made in that functional area. How might a computer system tie together some of those decisions and, in general, integrate the three decision making levels? What would that accomplish?

2. Select a number of the major operational level systems of one of the functional areas of a corporation (finance, manufacturing, etc.). Analyze the nature of those systems as being transaction driven, process oriented, etc., as described in this chapter. Do the different kinds of operational systems carry different kinds of computer processing requirements?

3. Repeat question 2 for tactical level systems with their corresponding types of computer programs: extractive, future time horizon, etc.

4. Do you think that a greater availability of information to middle and higher level managers, and the increased use of the computer for strategic and tactical decision making, will change the nature of the way that corporations are managed? Explain.

3

The Data Processing Environment

INTRODUCTION

In the early days of computing, the methodology of automated data processing was rather simple and limited: All of the processing took place in one room, and the computer ran just one program at a time. A program was loaded, accepted input from punched cards or magnetic tape, and produced output using a printer or a card punch. The processing was done strictly in "batch"—a large group of like-structured records was processed by one program. Random access to a single record was impossible.

In time, the technologies improved, and developments in hardware mushroomed. The fundamental processor and primary memory technology went from vacuum tubes to transistors to integrated circuits to larger scale integrated circuits. Secondary memory devices, especially magnetic disk devices, which provide the capability for random access to data, were developed and came into widespread use. Telecommunications, the technology for transmitting data over great or small distances, became a very important factor, with developments in satellite, microwave, cable, and other modes of transmission. A variety of new or vastly improved products emerged: printers, voice output devices, magnetic and optical character input devices, mass storage devices; the list goes on and on.

The developments in software were no less remarkable than those in hardware. High-level programming languages opened the door to an endless array of application development. Highly sophisticated operating systems, which many feel were even more of an achievement than the advanced hardware, were developed, often at great cost and by small armies of workers. Such systems became capable of allowing several programs to operate concurrently on a single processor, hundreds of programmers to develop programs simultaneously and in "real time," terminal operators to query a data bank concurrently, and different processors to share workloads and data storage units. Tools for managing data more efficiently, for generating applications in ways more efficient than by the standard use of even the best higher-level languages, and for planning and designing large programming projects, have all entered upon the scene and grown.

The result of the proliferation of hardware and software developments is an often bewildering, but highly sophisticated, array of choices

26

in data processing philosophies, methodologies, and environments today. In addition to processing a day's collected input to an application all in one batch, the individual items can be processed, as they are created, in real time. In addition to the arrangement of having all data processing done in one location, another option is to have it decentralized throughout many locations. It is now possible to have a distributed processing network, with processors and data banks at different locations, sharing the work load. Using specialized software systems, data can be arranged in highly nonredundant and interrelated ways. Finally, the current environment finds that job specialization in data processing has progressed to a fine level, with many separate disciplines in place.

REAL-TIME COMPUTING AND THE TERMINAL

The use of computers in a batch mode is merely an extension of the techniques used before computers. Typically analysts first studied the operations of the organization and then translated them from a manual mode to a fundamentally comparable computer mode. Processing was speeded up, cost increases were slowed, but business proceeded as usual. The computer revolution really began when terminals began to be placed on employees' desks.

Recording Changes as They Happen

With the introduction of the terminal into widespread use, the tasks to be carried out changed. It was possible to have all information related to the transaction available to the clerk at the time of data entry. The airline reservation operation when done by the travel agent is a good example of this shift. The time required to pick the best fare was decreased and many more options could be examined. Rapid customer service responses in such industries as utilities became a feasible exercise that no longer needed to consume hours of time.

Management control also changed in a significant way. The manufacturing process could now begin to keep track of every component and part being manufactured and assembled. This, almost by itself, began the reindustrialization of our plants. Higher levels of efficiency in inventory control and better scheduling of machines have the potential for tremendous savings. The manufacturing process has been changed by efficiencies that were only dreamt of previously.

Equally important is the effect on quality assurance in the manufacturing environment. A good real-time data collection process allows plant managers to detect problems early and to correct them. This added managerial capability saves both by minimizing rework and by eliminating many errors before they reach the public.

Interactive Programming

Programming has been one of the last operations to feel the pressure of automation. The key to bringing a major change into programming has been the interactive environment. The programmer now can interact directly with the system during the programming process. The same increase in efficiency that the other components of the organization gain by entering changes as they occur accrue also to the programmer. The programmer can now make a modification, test it (over and over), store the permanent change, document it, and enter the production environment all in one sitting. These new tools of the trade allow the programmer to improve the productivity of the programming task.

The Terminal as Everyone's Corporate Communications Link

The terminal will have its greatest effect in the area of communications. The electronic connection has made it possible to change the accepted relationships between control and geographical location. It was believed that a manager had to be able to see an employee each day to effectively control that employee's function. The immediacy of electronic communication and shared data are creating circumstances that are outside our normal realm of experience. The office automation furor is, in part, derived from an appreciation of the fact that we are entering uncharted territory when we create the possibility for massive electronic interconnection.

The perception that we are once more starting to swing, in pendulum-like fashion, toward centralization has been noted by observers. It appears that each generation of managers attempts to move away from the theory of its predecessors only to see its successors revert to the earlier approach. Whether the new communications environment will cause fundamental changes in the trend of reversing style every so often remains to be seen, however, the short term effects are likely to be exciting since they open many new possibilities.

CENTRALIZED/DECENTRALIZED

The issues of centralization and decentralization, as applied to data processing, have been in the forefront of much of the discussion[1] of the last decade. As users learned of the positive attributes of computers, they assumed that all the negative attributes derived from the fact that others controlled this scarce resource and that when they owned and controlled it, only good would be evident. This, of course, was a gross simplification of the problems that were occurring. The issue was interpreted as one of ownership of the equipment on which the programs ran. With the appearance of smaller mini- and microcomputers, the apparent problem grew to insurmountable levels as more and more departments acquired their own private computers, labeled for the accountants as tools, calculators, typewriters, or in some creative instances, toilet paper!

The issue was never really one of simple possession. Ownership of equipment opens up only a small part of the available possibilities. The computer centralization/decentralization issue has always been a stand-in for the more obvious issue of control. The owner of the hardware was presumed to control a certain portion of his or her destiny. "If I could wrest ownership from 'them,' then I would regain some portion of control over my private destiny." When the issue is described in simple control terms, then certain of the inconsistencies of a strict hardware view fall away.

Logical/Physical View

The image of a centralized environment that is most familiar to most of us begins with a room that contains most of our organization's data processing power. This room is off limits to all but the members of the data processing department who are responsible for the care and feeding of the equipment. These persons schedule the programs and operate the machines. The programmers who report to the data processing manager choose which programs are to be written soon and keep the programs that have already been written working to our benefit. In this view of a centralized facility, we think of a single physical location at which the resources are concentrated.

The conventional view of a decentralized environment imagines many smaller machines, each located at the place where the user resides. The user, operating his own equipment, is the source of the schedule that determines when each program will be run.

The distinguishing characteristic then, is the physical location of the equipment. This, however, is a misleading view. Consider, for example, an organization with many branch offices, each of which is the proud possessor of a computer. Each branch has an assigned clerk who reads a particular program into the computer every morning at 8:30 AM, and carries out a set of predefined acts during the day. Precisely at 4:30 PM this same clerk puts the machine to bed, again following a set of instructions from which he or she may not deviate.

Is this, then, a decentralized environment? Certainly not! The clerk's actions are totally constrained. The issue is control, not physical placement of the equipment.

In a similar sense, imagine a single large machine which each departmental group may access in an independent fashion. The access could be through a communications link or by personal delivery of the program to the computer center. Each department chooses when to deliver its program *and* when to enter it into the machine. Each department either writes its own program or pays to have its own program written. In this example, the physical centralization of the equipment is not equivalent to a centralization of control imposed on the using department.

There is a difference between the physical centralization of the equipment and the logical centralization of how access to that equipment is to be controlled. Figure 3.1 shows a 2 × 2 table in which the four combinations of logical and physical control are pictured. The traditional views described above are located in quadrants *a* and *d*. The counter example of physical centralization and logical decentralization is in quadrant *b* and the example of physical decentralization and logical centralization is in quadrant *c*.

In the view being put forward here, the differences between being

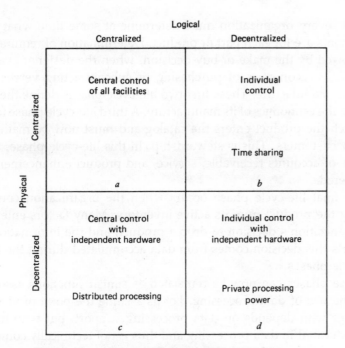

Figure 3.1. Logical and physical views of centralization.

centralized or decentralized become issues of control. In a centralized environment, a subordinate is assigned an objective *and* is told what to do to achieve that objective. In a decentralized environment, the subordinate is given a similar objective, but is also given freedom to choose the strategies and tactics to be used to achieve that objective. Clearly, if no objectives are given to a surbordinate, then control does not exist and we are describing an independent operation.

Multidimensional Control Spaces

The view presented above appears to concentrate on equipment while only hinting at other relationships associated with the issue of centralization/decentralization. This need not be the case. It is possible to separate[2] the treatment of equipment from the treatment of operations and systems implementation. A convenient model for this approach consists of viewing a product or part in a manufacturing environment in four life-cycle phases.

First, every organization must determine at some time what its requirements are for each part or product. Determination of requirements is followed by the make-or-buy decision, when the designer evaluates the relative economics of purchasing or subcontracting versus independent manufacture. These first two life-cycle phases define the product and the economics of its manufacture. A third life-cycle phase follows in which the product enters the catalog and must now be maintained for our customers. This is stewardship. In this life-cycle phase, all the aspects of accounts receivable, service, and product enhancements are considered.

The final life-cycle phase occurs when the organization considers retiring the product from its active inventory. Many factors enter in to an organization's decision to drop a product, and the information that supports this decision comes from data accumulated during the earlier life-cycle phases.

These phases can now be translated as similar functions associated with the use of data processing. Let us assume the point of view of a manager who depends on data processing support, but who has not been educated in data processing and thus is not technically competent to be a data processing professional. This manager can still control the use and allocation of data processing just as he can control the allocation and use of copiers and communication networks without being able to physically change their behavior. In this view it is not necessary to have one department responsible for an application in each of its life-cycle phases; control may be separated and assigned to the department which can do the job best.

The first of the life-cycle phases—in which we determine our requirements for something—translates into an ability to determine what computers should be used for. This decision is equivalent to setting priorities for different projects to determine the sequence of their computer implementation.

The make/buy decision assumes that we have determined what we need to reach our objectives and we must now select the appropriate vehicle for acquiring the program. *Make* would imply that we, ourselves, manage the process of producing the program, whereas *acquire* implies that we subcontract the job to a vendor who may or may not be a member of our parent organization. In data processing terms, this represents systems implementation.

When a product has been completed, it is then our responsibility to maintain it throughout its useful life. During stewardship of a working data processing system, someone is responsible for providing adequate service on a scheduled basis. This responsibility includes choosing the times at which the program will run, operating the equipment while it is running, and keeping the function performed reasonably up to date.

The last of the life-cycle phases, retirement, is rarely applied to a data processing system because data processing is so young. Most of our applications are still in their first generation. The steps necessary to replace a useful, fully operational system would be complex, and no thorough methods have been worked out to deal with this situation. Yet one could conceivably imagine this phase to be one aspect of the determination of requirements decision.[3]

These components describe a set of tasks that may be separated and done independently. If we think of the physical location of equipment as equivalent to the stewardship or facilities management of a product, then the logical location of the equipment may be equivalent to product ownership—controlling what will be done with the equipment or deciding which application shall be done next and which will run on the equipment. In this view, then, a third dimension can be similarly defined in which the implementation of the software system becomes the third axis of a control geometry. Each of these axes, systems selection, system implementation, and system operation, can be either locally controlled or centrally controlled. There are then eight control possibilities available. This concept can be extended by separating software from hardware, data from program, or even operational control from informational and tool programs.

The issue of whether to centralize or decentralize is then a complex issue if all the possibilities are rationally considered. The choice, in the final analysis, may be independent of any of these rational concerns. The style of each organization will determine a tendency toward one of the two extremes, and all technical considerations may be irrelevant when the choice is made.

Advantages/Disadvantages

There are many lists of advantages and disadvantages associated with these two organizational styles. Most of the items assume some technical model of equipment or program for justification. If we choose to be independent of technology, then the core distinction between the two styles is the difference between local optimization and global optimization.

Local optimization assumes that a choice can be made by an individual to optimize his or her environment. Alternatives can be ranked in such a way that the individual's most pressing concerns can be met.

Global optimization assumes that an organization can maximize its complete good by trading off concerns among some smaller components. It may mean that one group waits for a locally crucial item while the rest do even more globally crucial operations. Local responsiveness is traded for organizational efficiency with its bureaucratic overhead.

Centralization seems to work best in those instances when the cost of bureaucracy does not outweigh the gains obtained from a single integrated direction. Decentralization works best when the complexity of a particular activity would require a high level of bureaucracy if it were centralized. The cost of the bureaucracy then exceeds the savings associated with a single integrated approach.

Electronics, then, seems to support both directions. On the one hand, it allows for tighter control via communication links, and on the other, it allows for looser control by permitting information to be placed in the hands of the remote manager.

DISTRIBUTED PROCESSING

The term *distributed processing* has had much use in the past decade. It has been described in a manner that is synonymous with decentralized approaches and that assumes that in all instances when equipment is placed away from a single home site, a distributed environment has been created. The word itself implies that a single function is somehow broken up into several pieces, with one component here and the other there. This does describe the environment; however, in those instances when a piece is broken into several components, a control relationship still exists between them. As shown in Figure 3.1, distribution occurs when there is physical decentralization and logical centralization. Quadrant *d* in Figure 3.1, both physical and logical decentralization, represents independent processing sites and does not describe what the literature has begun to call distributed processing.

Advantages/Disadvantages

Distributed processing allows management to reassert control in those instances where accidents of geography or of differing functions have forced a headquarters group to allow some local autonomy or independence. The bureaucratic measures would have been too expensive. With electronic connections, remote management becomes possible. Information can flow through an electronic pipe and be made available to managers quickly. Control can be reasserted because of commonly available files. Thus, distributed processing has led to a trend toward recentralizing control of our multinational organizations. The issue of local initiative still represents a tangible set of advantages for decentralizing some environments in those cases where the flavor, tone, and sense of a problem can not be translated into data to be distributed along the electronic umbilical cord.

Finally, logical decentralization makes sense where the complexity of an area is such that we only confuse the issue when we try to consider it in its more global perspective. In these instances we allow random market forces to help stabilize an independent organization's relationship to the rest of the structure.

DATABASE

Description

Using the broadest possible definition, a company's database is its collection of machine-processable data. Actually, the term has come to have a more technically limited and precise meaning: A database is a collection of data that can be simultaneously shared by multiple users. It can store data in a nonredundant fashion while easily allowing complex retrievals of the data, based on semantic interrelationships.

To manage access to the database, a complex piece of software called a database management system (DBMS) is needed. All program and query accesses to the database must pass through and be controlled by the DBMS. The DBMS requires that the data be stored in some particular structure and that accesses to the data be posed in some particular form. Certain standard kinds of data management concerns, such as security, backup and recovery, concurrency (the problem of simultaneous update by multiple users), and auditability are also the DBMS's responsibility.

Several other terms, functions, and products have become a part of the database milieu. *Data* (or database) *administration* refers to the human function responsible for managing the data in the database (and, often, other data too). A *data dictionary* is a set of files that documents the nature of the data in the database. *Database design* refers to the set of decisions made concerning the precise form that the data will take, given the constraints of the data structure allowed by the DBMS. Various software utilities predict and monitor the performance of the DBMS-centered systems. Others are concerned with the storage space used, the security of the data, and the use of the data for accounting purposes. *Distributed database* refers to a system in which the data is scattered, possibly redundantly, at different sites on a distributed network, and yet, as far as the programmers are concerned, functions as if it were a centralized database system. A *database machine* is a piece of hardware that off-loads the actual data retrieval function from the computer's central processor.

Because data is a central theme of this book, we will have much more to say about all of these items later.

Advantages/Disadvantages

There are several clear and compelling advantages to the database approach. Data is increasingly being thought of as a significant corporate resource. New data management techniques, centered around the database approach, are needed to make that concept work. Databases allow data to be held in a nonredundant fashion. They allow complex interrelationships of data to be exploited. They handle the security, backup and recovery, and concurrency chores. They produce a more data-independent environment—one in which changes to the data structure cause less havoc to programs already written and operating.

The disadvantages of the database approach, in most situations, are far outweighed by the advantages. There are two main disadvantages. One is that the complexity of the database environment may have a detrimental effect on a given database program's performance. The other is that the environment may require a higher level of personnel skills. For certain very specific situations, such as airline reservations systems, the performance issue is a valid one. But in general, companies today cannot afford to *not* adopt the database approach.

PERSONNEL

As the use of computers has grown, one question that has occasionally arisen is whether mass automation would lead to mass unemployment. While the question is still subject to controversy, it is clear that a variety of new job categories has been created in the computer field, and a wide variety of other personnel use computers to some degree in their work.

Computer Professionals

The major, full-time job categories in data processing are programmer, systems analyst, computer operator, and computer repairman.

In general, a programmer's job is to encode application requirements in a type of language that can be translated into intstructions that a computer can act on. Actually, that description fits the most common kind of programmer, the "application programmer." The more senior application programmers (sometimes called "lead programmers") may be involved in designing strategies for major programming efforts, including deciding how the job should be subdivided among the other application programmers. Another kind of programmer, known as a systems programmer, is concerned with the maintenance, installation, and tuning of the so-called system control programs, which are massive pieces of software that manage the application programs and the hardware. A third kind of programmer, which we might loosely call a "development programmer," would typically work for a computer manufacturer or software development firm and would write system control and related software.

A systems analyst's job is quite different from a programmer's, although a move from programmer to systems analyst is often considered a promotional path through a data processing organization. Unfortunately, since the skills required for the two jobs are quite different, such

job changes do not always work out all that well. The systems analyst
is concerned primarily with the beginning of the application development cycle. It is his job to interview the people responsible for the
business process that is to be automated, to review the appropriate
documentation on it, and then to document it in a form which will allow
the programmers to actually implement it. Thus the systems analyst
should have as part of his background both a general understanding of
how the company's business functions and a moderate understanding
of data processing. To be effective, he must have a personality that
permits him to work well with other people. He must be able to deal
with the end users on a nontechnical basis and then turn around and
talk to the data processing personnel in highly technical and analytical
terms.

Computer operators are responsible for running the data processing
hardware. The skills required vary from relatively simple, such as
mounting tapes on tape drives, to relatively complex, such as monitoring
an operating system's workings at the central processor console. Operators, as opposed to programmers and analysts, usually do not have
college degrees. Nevertheless, many of them work their way up to
programming as a next career step.

Hardware repairmen, also known as "field engineers" or "customer
engineers," are the people who actually fix the computer hardware
when it breaks down. Those who have college backgrounds tend to be
electrical engineers. As systems grow more advanced, the relationship
between hardware and software becomes quite integrated, and customer
engineers assume responsibility for certain aspects of software systems
too.

Other Information-Processing Workers

A variety of other either less common or lower-level job specialties can
be listed. The most familiar of the lower-level workers are the data entry
personnel. Their work, which is closely related to that of the typist, is
to repetitively convert nonmachine data into machine-processable data.
At one time these were the industry's "keypunch operators," punching
data into the ubiquitous punched cards. Now, many key data directly
onto tapes or disks, using more modern equipment.

Some examples of less common, professional positions are as follows:

Several new job categories have been created under the umbrella of "data administration." All are in some way concerned with managing the data in a company's database and, in many cases, other data too. Specific titles include data analyst, database systems programmer, and data dictionary specialist. In addition, there is a specialty within the data communications area concerned with the transmission of data. Another position is that of "planner." Planners forecast the organization's future hardware and software needs. A final example is the data processing auditor, who insures the integrity and security of the data and the processing environment.

In general, when we think of information-processing workers and their allied peers, we must increasingly keep in mind the image of all of the support personnel that any business department requires. There will be parallel jobs created in data processing to perform similar functions. The scope of computers has grown to so great an extent that a simple categorization of specialties no longer suffices. Some even depend on the business that we are in.

The Computer and Noncomputer People

The computer has touched the working lives of a phenomenal number of people in all types of business activities. Such contact can only increase as time goes on. A few examples will illustrate the point.

The earliest, large-scale business use of the computer was in accounting. The high-volume, repetitive tasks lent themselves well, in a cost effective way, to the capabilities of the computer. Today the computer has largely relieved the accountant of those repetitive tasks and allows him to concentrate on the more esoteric problems of his profession.

Airline reservation clerks spend their entire working time in front of a computer terminal. Today, flight information is retrieved and reservations are made on an on-line basis.

Automobile designers have been able to replace much of their sketching and model building with three-dimensional computer graphic representations. Modifying the design, which would otherwise be an annoyingly laborious process, is greatly simplified on a graphic terminal.

And outside of the work environment, everyone has come into contact with computing technology in one way or another. From telephone bills to home video games; from credit card and bank statements to personal computers, the list is endless and will only increase as time goes on.

The Computer and the Manager

All managers make decisions. To make a good decision, a manager needs certain pertinent information to supplement his experience and intuition. The higher the manager's level, the farther from his immediate grasp is the information with which he can make an informed decision.

One of the effects that computers have is to provide more (but, one hopes, not too much) information to managers at various levels for their decision-making needs. The information can take the form of printed reports or of on-line data, flashing up on demand on the manager's video terminal. One interesting effect of this phenomenon is that, in some cases, very high-level executives have begun taking a more active role in the management of their suboperations. They used to be content to leave such matters to their subordinates, but now, for the first time, they have the pertinent data on an instantaneous, up-to-the-minute basis, and so are inclined to take a more active role.

REFERENCES

1. Akoka, J., "Centralization Versus Decentralization of Information Systems: A Critical Survey and an Annotated Bibliography," *CISR Report*, Sloan School of Management, MIT, Cambridge, MA, 1977.
2. Rockart, J. F., Bullen, C. V., and Kegan, J. N., "The Management of Distributed Processing," *CISR Report*, Sloan School of Management, MIT, Cambridge, MA, 1978.
3. "Replacing Old Applications," *EDP Analyzer*, Vol. 21, No. 3, 1983.

QUESTIONS FOR THOUGHT

1. We are approaching an era when a large percentage of a corporation's personnel will have a computer terminal on their desks. Those terminals will allow their users to communicate with each other and to access appropriate data stored in the corporate data bases. Choose a particular corporate occupation and describe how the new environment will affect employees in that occupation in terms of:

a. The way that they perform their job.

b. The way that they communicate with others in the organization.

c. The way that their managers oversee their work.

d. The skills that they need to perform their job.

2. Choose a particular industry and assume that there is a company in that industry whose information processing is centralized and that there is another company in it whose information processing is decentralized. Compare the two companies in terms of:

a. The ways in which they organize their data.

b. The ways in which top management utilize data for strategic decision making.

c. The ways in which accountants audit the companies.

d. The ways in which the data processing departments organize application development.

3. Consider all of the advances in data processing mentioned in this chapter and speculate on the types of jobs, the relative numbers of people in those jobs, and the skill required for those jobs, in five, ten, and twenty years from now.

The Solution Process and Alternative Methods

4

The Four Phases of Planning Through Design

BUSINESS STRATEGIC PLANNING

Corporate Goals

The success or failure of corporations seems to depend on a mixture of sorcery, luck, inspiration, and attention to detail. Each of these facets has been pointed at in any given organization's past to explain its ability to survive some particularly difficult situation. Sorcery, luck, and inspiration seem to be outside the usual control of most of us, and thus it would appear at first that well-run organizations can at best only control attention to detail.

If this is the correct combination of the attributes that account for success, then good planning would seem to have a rather small area of application, and why would anyone even consider wasting their time on such a thankless piece of drudgery? The proper response to this kind of thinking is to explain the role of strategic planning and corporate goals in the overall scheme of things.

Sorcery, luck, and inspiration are the essence of strategic planning. Knowing where it makes sense to look, which areas are crucial to your future, and which rabbits need to be pulled out of the hat depend on being prepared for eventualities. If you are not positioned to take into account some lucky happening, then you are not lucky. You have to be there. If you don't have someone who knows the "vocabulary" of an area of interest, you will not be credibly inspired. If there are no rabbits in the hat, then nothing can be pulled out.

Strategic planning at the corporate level, then, requires the planners to narrow down the focus of concern so that no unnecessary effort is expended in working for that which cannot be achieved. This means that the job of strategic planning involves two essential components. The first understands what can be done and sets reasonable objectives, and the second gets the rabbits ready if they are needed.

The objectives that a good strategic planning system works with identifies the targets that we need to pursue to be lucky. The characteristics of these objectives need to be understood in the light of luck, sorcery, and inspiration. We need to be involved in each of the potential areas that seem to be in our focus of operation to the extent that as changes appear over the horizon, we always seem to be prepared to advance on the best of them and retreat from the worst of them. This is a difficult task. The major failing of strategic objectives is one of scope. They have a tendency to overspecify areas that are understood and to pass with a wave of the hand those least understood. This is a common failing in any level of planning or design and guarantees that as an organization we will always be prepared for yesterday's problems to the exclusion of tomorrow's challenges. The setting of reasonable strategic objectives, general enough to be pertinent and tight enough to avoid useless effort, is thus a significant organizational talent.

Long-Term versus Short-Term Plans

The planning horizon that we use in strategic planning depends on the rate of change of our environment. When we are interested in specific operations to help us in our daily activities, the short-term plan seems to be in control. When we are concerned with trends and evolving market forces, we are concerned with long-term planning. There is no razor's edge that divides the two time spans. There is, however, a different approach that is applied in the short-term. Specificity is the characteristic of the short-term plan. It contains actions and their expected results, and we expect that the relationships that the plan predicts will in fact come to pass. On the other hand, the long-term plan is characterized by breadth of view and preparation. The long-term plan must identify those forces that will come to pass that we must take into account in great detail. The long-term plan prepares us; the short-term plan directs us.

INFORMATION SYSTEMS STRATEGIC PLANNING

Information systems are the means with which the information we need to run an organization is effectively collected and delivered. Information systems budgets are growing each year, and the function is progressively gathering more daily and long-term operations under its wings. This means that the relative importance of information systems to management will continue to grow. The data processing change is somewhat analogous to the change in thinking that cost accounting has fostered within manufacturing. Whenever a tool of this level of importance appears, its effective use must be planned for. It is a scarce resource that needs to be made available to the group that can benefit from it most.

There are two views of the way data processing can be used in organizations. The first view accepts computers as defensive weapons. They are the means by which exploding cost spirals in administration are tamed and by which information required to improve the efficiency of production processes is gathered and then applied, and the source of reports which management uses to find and demonstrate its insight into the workings of the organization. In this view, the operating budget of each department is sensitive to the amount of resources and expense the computer supplies. In this view, management allocates this resource wisely based on a planning process that takes into account individual performance and its effect on the bottom line.

A different view includes data processing among the offensive weapons of the organization. It makes possible new products that would be unheard of without its capabilities. The offensive weapon can be unleashed, for example, to improve service by its superior ability to make information available.

These two points of view alter the location of computers in the planning process. When computers are viewed as defensive tools, their applicable horizon contracts; when they are viewed as offensive weapons, their planning horizon moves further out. In either view the goals of the organization depend on the ability of data processing to deliver a particular type of service at a particular level of availability.

Supporting the Business Strategic Plans

When an organization's view of data processing changes to the extent that it becomes a part of the complete planning process, the planners start to look at strategic opportunities made possible by enhanced capabilities. This represents the first step in a mature inclusion of information systems into the business planning process. When the planning community becomes comfortable with including data processing in their thought process, they start to take it for granted, and it can become a natural part of the strategic planning process. The thought process then becomes one in which "ideal," desired objectives are identified, the assumed environment in which they can be achieved is sketched, and the specific programs (with a small p) required to achieve these goals are specified. Electronic processing capability can then be said to support business strategic goals.

Information Systems Goals

The information systems management team has its own strategic planning responsibility. Each of the reasons and techniques described above has its parallel in information systems planning. Just as success in business strategic planning can be said to depend on sorcery, luck, inspiration, and attention to detail, so too success in information systems planning can be said to depend on the same factors. For some of us the amount of sorcery is at a continuously high level.

However, all of these attributes have the same strategic insight at their root. The trick for information systems management is to be able to forecast in an extremely fast-changing technological environment. The paths to success in each type of planning are the same. There is no essential difference between successful business planning and successful systems planning. Objectives must be set, early warning systems established, and personnel nurtured. If the information systems management has failed, it has done so because of a lack of training in general management principals and the false belief that systems are somehow different from supertankers, skyscrapers, or mergers and stock offerings.

Plans to Achieve the Information Systems Goals

The effective information systems organization must have a symbiotic sharing of organizational goals with the other operating departments. Since these operating departments represent the real goods and services delivered by the organization, they should lead the way. True, they are responsible for making certain that the direction in which they are heading can be supported by the information systems group, but in any event, their priorities should be dominant.

The strategic planning role of the information systems group is to be aware of that which will be possible tomorrow and to educate the operating groups about the functions that will be practicable and therefore that ought to enter into planning considerations. This combination of responsibilities is not unique to information systems. It is true of all the disciplines that are needed to make a product. What is unique is the newness of computers and their continued rapid rate of change. That is all the more reason why they must be included in long-term strategic planning.

DETAILED SYSTEMS ANALYSIS

Systems analysis is the term that has traditionally been applied to the first major phase of the *data processing application development cycle*, whose elements are listed below.

1. Systems analysis.
2. Systems and database design.
3. Implementation.
4. Testing.
5. Installation.
6. Maintenance.

Systems analysis normally encompasses a number of procedures and a number of goals, all directed toward making an organized start in the development of a new application. Precisely what systems analysis entails varies with the circumstances of the particular application and the way that a company's application development personnel have tailored the process to suit their needs.

Broadly stated, systems analysis is the action of studying a business process and describing it in a manner that can be used to develop an automated data processing application to accomplish or aid in the execution of that business process. It can include a feasibility study to determine whether the application and the development process are viable in terms of the expense involved, the personnel needed, the computer hardware needed, and the complexity of the business process itself. It can also include a cost–benefit analysis to insure that the value of the computer application is not lost in the development, execution, and maintenance costs. But the primary function of systems analysis is to provide an interface between those people (the "end users") responsible for the business process, and the data processing personnel who will attempt to automate it.

The essence of systems analysis is transformation: the conversion of the knowledge of how a business process works from the terms used by user personnel to the terms familiar to data processing personnel. The person responsible for that conversion is the systems analyst. To be successful, a systems analyst must, of course, have a firm grasp of an appropriate set of tools. But he should also be comfortable in dealing with a variety of people, and should have at least a general understanding of the organization's business and operational methods.

The systems analyst begins his job by studying the business process, reading the documentation that has been written about it, interviewing the personnel responsible for it, and learning about any existing automated systems used for it. He then must convert all of that acquired knowledge into a form that will eventually be given to the systems and database designers as input to their tasks. Note that the created description of the business process should be geared only toward describing how the process works and not toward how it might be implemented on data processing equipment.

But the process is not quite that direct. It is virtually inconceivable, given the complexities and uncertainties involved, that the systems analyst's first written description of the business process will entirely accurately reflect how the process in fact functions. The key to success in this endeavor is feedback. The form in which the systems analyst writes the process description must be understandable to the end user. Then the procedure becomes one of continual refinement of the systems analyst's description through consultation with the end user.

The systems analyst's description of the business process will become the blueprint for both the systems (or program) designers and the database designers. While the form of the description has to be understandable to the end users for feedback purposes, it must also be sufficiently precise and detailed for those data processing professionals who will use it in the continuation of the application development cycle. To repeat a point made in an earlier chapter, a sound job of systems analysis is absolutely essential to a well-planned and error-resistant application development cycle.

It becomes clear, too, that the systems analyst, or group of systems analysts, who investigates and documents a varied set of business processes, is in a position to develop an unrivaled understanding of how the business, as a whole, works. They have studied the individual parts of the company in detail and have spoken with a wide variety of people about the nature of their jobs. Furthermore, they have documented all of that acquired knowledge, using a common, universally applicable and understandable technique.

Such a compendium of how the entire organization, or even parts of it, functions can also be considered to be a universal guide to how the organization operates. Strategic-level management can use such a guide in understanding the functioning of the overall organization and how the various parts interact. It can be an invaluable aid in planning for future organizational changes. Tactical-level management can also use the systems analysis documentation as a plan in managing their particular part of the company. In addition they can use it to manage their responsibilities in terms of interactions with other parts of the company. Operational management can use it as a reference for fulfilling responsibilities at a detailed level.

DATABASE DESIGN

One aspect of developing an application system is designing the structures in which the data will be stored. Within the constraints of the kinds of structures allowed by the particular database management system that has been chosen, the database designer must decide which data fields should be grouped together to form records and files and how those record types and files should be related or connected to each other (if at all). That process is known as "database design."

Database design always begins with a list of the data fields to be used in the database and a thorough understanding of their meanings, including their relationships to each other. Beyond this, there are several key factors that must be considered in the process, including security considerations, query frequency, response-time requirements, and, usually, a multitude of performance-oriented items peculiar to the particular data storage system involved.

There are several reasons why a careful job of database design is crucial to the well-being of an application system. First, in a broad sense, is the proposition that a company's stored data is increasingly looked on as a manageable resource to be shared by all appropriate company personnel. It is clear that under these circumstances, an orderly, intelligent design is necessary both from a managerial point of view and a mutual performance optimization point of view. In addition, there are three main technical points.

1. *Data Redundancy.* The form of data storage must be designed in such a way that redundancy among the stored data items is eliminated or kept to a bare minimum. Redundancy is the bane of stored data. Redundant data takes up extra space on the storage devices. It takes that much more time to update data if they appear in several places than if they only appear in one place. Even if one attempts to update redundant data, the chances are quite high that from time to time, through machine or human error, an update will be successfully performed on some, but not all of the copies of a redundantly held data item. Thus the database becomes inconsistent and not worthy of trust.

2. *Multiple Associations.* Sometimes a piece of data of one kind relates to several pieces of data of another kind; for instance, a manager has several employees, or an assembly is made of several parts. It is very important to take such associations into account in designing data bases. The ability to accurately represent the real world depends on it.

3. *Data Independence.* The term *data independence* refers to the ability to change the stored form of a set of data items without affecting programs that have already been written that use that data. The database designer must strive for the greatest level of data independence within the constraints of the data storage system. Clearly, the dynamic nature of application systems makes the addition of new data types in the future inevitable, new data that may well have relationships with existing data. In fact, new relationships between existing data may be needed by new applications. The goal, in working toward· data independence, is to be able to accommodate such changes without affecting existing applications.

THE CONTINUOUS-FLOW APPROACH

Introduction

We have said that business strategic planning is critical to a company's well being and growth. We have also made the point that since an information system is so central and important a support mechanism in increasingly many ways, information systems strategic planning is a natural, and very necessary, follow-on to business strategic planning.

Independently, we have made a case for detailed systems analysis and database design as crucial steps in the creation of data processing application systems.

The next question to ask is, if there is a strong connection between business strategic planning and information systems strategic planning, is there a connection between the latter and detailed systems analysis and/or database design? The answer is a resounding "yes," and, indeed, serves as a central theme of this book.

The Interfaces Among Planning, Analysis, and Design

Information systems strategic planning and detailed systems analysis both involve planning for application systems implementation. Both require a certain (albeit often different) degree of knowledge about the way a company and various business processes in it function. The same remark can be made regarding the data involved in the applications. The differences between the two levels required are a matter of scope of interest and degree of detail. In information systems strategic planning, the scope is very large—the entire company or a major portion of it—whereas the degree of detail that the study must go into is relatively slight. In detailed systems analysis the scope is relatively small—one or a small set of specific applications—but the level of detail is great.

It follows that the output from information systems strategic planning can be divided into parts and each part used as input to a detailed systems analysis effort. After all, a particular portion of the output from information systems strategic planning really represents, at a relatively modest level of detail, the information about the business processes and data requirements for a related set of data processing applications.

In a search for relationships among the component operations, it becomes clear that there is a strong interface between detailed systems analysis and database design. Actually, as we move from detailed systems analysis into the design stage of an application development cycle, the effort forks into two processes. One is program design, the act of deciding how best to construct programs to accomplish the processing needed to satisfy the requirements as stated in the detailed systems analysis output. The other is database design.

It is quite clear that a portion of the output of detailed systems analysis is a list of the set of fields needed by the application(s) and a list of the relationships among them. It is just as clear that that very same knowledge is what is required as input to the database design process.

The Continuous-Flow Approach

Information systems strategic planning, detailed systems analysis, and database design are, unfortunately, not always practiced seriously or competently in many organizations. Sometimes they are not practiced at all. But in those companies in which they are actively employed, a frequent stumbling block regards the method of smoothly stepping from one process to the next. The transition from business strategic planning to information systems strategic planning is clear. But can there be a smooth operational flow from information systems strategic planning to detailed systems analysis to database design?

It is our contention that not only can there be such a smooth flow, but there *must* be to achieve the best information processing system possible.

The continuous flow from information systems strategic planning to detailed systems analysis to database design follows from the consideration in all three of the data involved and of the understanding of how the business processes under consideration work. In information systems strategic planning a broad view of both the data and the business processes is taken. That view is explored in much greater depth, for particular applications, in detailed systems analysis. Finally, in database design, the data fields, based on their meanings and relationships as defined by the business processes, are organized into a machine-processable database.

The flow from business strategic planning to database design is a series of steps in which description and elucidation follow each other. The literature is replete with an array of different approaches to each of the phases of organizational uses of computers. There are no guidelines associated with the relationship between approaches as you procede through each of the phases that a good job of planning necessitates. The mental process that helps to choose which technique is applicable to a particular organization is a pendulum swinging back and forth between description and elucidation. In description, the systems analyst answers the question *why;* in elucidation the analyst answers the question *how.* Two different businessmen may find themselves in different business environments, implying different needs in the study of the nature of their businesses. Their need to analyze the *why* is different. Both understand the need to elucidate and expand on how an objective is to be met, but because they start with different initial needs, their techniques will be different. They have a continuous-flow approach, with similar results, even though they may use alternative ways of arriving at the final system.

The disconcerting feeling that arises from viewing these three steps as unconnected operations is needless. A well-run data processing organization that has strong management commitment to spend adequate time in the planning stages of application development should recognize the smooth and important transitions in moving from one of these steps to the next. Fundamentally they all involve the maintenance and transformation of data, guided by the ways that the business processes that use and generate that data work.

QUESTION FOR THOUGHT

1. If the essence of planning involves being prepared for the future how can an organization determine when it has done enough work? Can you suggest some guidelines and stopping rules for the workings of a planning department?

5

Business Strategic Planning: Concepts and Needs

In the previous chapter we introduced the idea of strategic planning and its purpose within the organization. In this chapter we shall try to specify more of the details of strategic planning at the headquarters level.

OBJECTIVES AND FOCUS

Strategic planning has the potential for being a very useful tool for insuring the continued growth of an organization. However, it is easy to turn a strategic planning exercise into wishful thinking, which is not only useless but dangerous and counterproductive. The key to avoiding negative consequences is to understand the relationship between the focus of your organization and the objectives that you establish for it.

"Focus," an idea introduced by Black,[1] represents the area where your natural growth should occur because it is an extension of current products and falls within the expertise of your personnel. An understanding of your focus requires an awareness of the trends of the environment as expressed by your natural "growth vector" and the internal business factors that affect your current and expected position within your industry.

Focus thus represents your view of yourself, together with the public's expectation of your strong points. If a computer manufacturer attempted to market shoes in competition with established shoe manufacturers, it would probably fail. Conglomerates succeed when the acquired, diverse company is managed as an independent unit, with its retained name and trademarks.

Objectives, on the other hand, represent that which the strategic planner believes can be accomplished. Usually objectives are viewed as having three attributes: they are "actionable," achievable, and measurable. These attributes tend to rule out the situation in which objectives are treated as unattainable targets to shoot for. That approach to strategic planning does not work because although a direction may be established, few people work up to their potential—they know that they are not expected to achieve any particular result.

An objective is "actionable" if it is assigned to an individual or group who have it in their power to affect the action taken. A salesperson who is assigned a quota must be able to reach those people capable of making

58

a sales decision about the appropriate products. If the territorial assignment specifically excludes that salesperson from making calls on decision makers capable of ordering products, then that salesperson will sit back and wait for fate to intervene. On the other hand, if one's actions directly affect the ability to achieve one's quota, then one will work very hard to achieve that quota *providing* one believes that there is a chance that it is possible. This is the second attribute of an objective; it must be achievable, or at least perceived as being reachable.

The third attribute of an objective is that it must be capable of being measured. If an objective cannot be expressed in terms that are capable of being measured, then it is impossible to determine if it has been reached. It is often quite difficult to establish a measurement system sufficiently sensitive to determine whether the subjective goals that seem to be significant have in fact been achieved.

ROLE OF STRATEGIC PLANNING IN THE ORGANIZATION

Strategic planning has two faces. It looks outwards in an attempt to understand the environment and its role in that environment, and it looks inwards to understand what the organization and its employees are capable of achieving. These are not easy tasks, *know thyself* and *know thy neighbor* both require continued refinement and study.

This is a different approach than viewing planning as a set of detailed steps that work out to accomplish a particular goal. To the extent that a plan is documented, it can be used to refine the next plan and the planning process. In a real sense strategic planning is a probe inserted into the innards of the organization, measuring its responses to specific stimuli. Strategic planning, when well documented and done continuously, measures the "brain" that directs the organization. The ability to improve the way an organization achieves its strategic planning objectives implies that it is learning about its powers and therefore is in better control of its destiny. The essence of strategic planning is to guarantee survival to repeat the exercise again.

Reaction to Change

Strategic planning and long-range planning were begun because environments change. To make some slack time and provide for adequate response, organizations began to predefine their actions in some well-specified scenarios. The slack time is required because competitive circumstances forced each organization to respond at the rate of the most agile of their group. The requirement to be able to respond quickly is closely linked to the rate of change of several attributes: social pressures, technological pressures, and political pressures. When these are all stagnant, then no change occurs and hence little strategic planning is necessary. That is not to say that long-range planning is eliminated since any behemoth must consider the location of its next step very carefully simply because of its size. The telephone industry in the United States, in the years following the Second World War, illustrated this relationship. Shielded from competition, regulated by the government providing a fixed rate of return, depreciating equipment over decades, the phone company did not plan new markets but did plan for orderly equipment transitions in the depreciation time schedule allotted to them. This experience, common to most industries a score or so years ago, however, has changed.

The Changing Environment

The rate of change of technology today is spurring changes in the social and political arenas. At one time it was assumed that the time delay between application and discovery was of the order of 20 years. Today that time delay is being sliced down dramatically. In the area of microelectronics, for example, two or three years separate major shifts in products such as calculators and watches. In a recent book on strategic management, Ansoff[2] stresses the effect of environmental turbulence on the strategic planning process. Two countervailing forces are pitted against each other in some segments of industry. The first is technological change, and the second is the increase in the time required to make an adequate response to an unexpected innovation. Ansoff hypothesizes that organizations have responded to this apparently contradictory state of affairs by generating a process of organizational learning. The tool that organizations use to perform the research on their environments to determine what information ought to be accumulated is the planning process.

In this mental model it appears that an analogy is being made between technology advancement and organizational survival. Strategic planning plays the role of basic research. Specialists in a given area try to extend the state of knowledge by theory and experimentation. Organizational strategists follow growth vectors and strengths to predict and document trends and then compare that which is predicted with what has occurred.

At the next level engineers develop practical applications from insights gained by basic research; long-range planners, looking at strategic plans, start to develop the details of how some of the objectives identified can be obtained. These long-range planners start to accumulate the resources and knowledge required to bring the strategic goals to fruition.

At the next level the manufacturing engineers begin to design the process by which a cost-effective usable product can be manufactured; short-range planners working from 6 months to 18 month intervals, do operational planning.

Finally a product is marketed, delivered, and supported by the operational staff who are required to track it for quality and for acceptance so that the process can be improved. This last set of steps when associated with the planning process should coincide with the business operations process. For the analogy to be completed, the rest of the steps have to be made to coincide also. In the same manner that a good technology-based organization must structure some form of connecting information system across the boundaries of the four phases, so too must any organization build a set of connecting disciplines that span the four organizational interfaces. In the engineering professions the term used to describe these connecting links is *configuration management*. This is what is needed in the planning environments.

TECHNICAL

The increased rate of change of technology, already mentioned, works hand in hand with social and political pressures. Sometimes technology drives change; sometimes politics and society force technological innovation. The difference between the environmental turbulence of the eighties and the fifties is that the changes occur more quickly.

It is easy to give examples where well-established industries were rudely awakened by technological innovation. The introduction of digital watches shook the established manufacturers. Thus the watchmaking business is in the process of immense pendulum-like changes. Electronics was capable of providing the accuracy of the best Swiss watchmakers at throw-away prices, and consumers responded to both the novelty and the additional functions made available.

The result has been to turn watch manufacturing into what appears to be two separate and distinct industries. One for the general consumer overlaps the calculator market, and the other, designed for the luxury trade, is making old-style analog watches a unique expensive item. The shake-out is eliminating all but the best-run and *luckiest* of the original entrepreneurs.

That brings to mind the old saying, "How can you tell the pioneers?, They are the ones with arrows in their backs!" There are two possible morals one can learn from this saying: either never be first, watch the leaders, and be ready to take over the minute they identify the opposition, or, if you must be a pioneer (and to the successful pioneers fall the greatest successes), always scout out the territory before charging down the mountain.

POLITICAL

The second force that is increasing the pace of change is political. The will of society as expressed in political goals is having a very strong effect on the destiny of today's organizations. When public action groups persuade many people of the relative goodness of a particular product feature, organizations caught napping can be dealt an expensive blow. The automobile manufacturers "discovered" safety as a key requirement of their products only after the public had been educated in its necessity. The cigarette manufacturers were forced into product innovation and alternate manufacturing media after Congress believed the medical research reports coming from respected sources.

These political effects are on the national stage. On the international stage, the OPEC intervention in the oil market caused a violent restructuring of all aspects of the process of bringing petroleum products to the market place and created a favorable mood for introducing various alternative supplies of energy. Those that could take advantage of the sudden shift in the political wind were able to capitalize on the changed direction.

Closer to the subject of this book is the view of data as a national resource that is being stressed by some of the European countries. In this view, the information used by multinational corporations to plan their own organization's future becomes subject to government control. If the host governments view this data as a treasure not to be moved without permission, then the organization that generated the same data ought to plan for its orderly use.

Political action, even when taken indirectly, can cause tremendous change in an organization. Simple tax law changes absorb much spare programming capacity each year. There are many such changes that occur each year, affecting the full spectrum of an organization's operations. These are excellent examples of the type of environmental turbulence that is totally unexpected, yet must be prepared for if the current level of survival is to be guaranteed for any organization.

SOCIAL

The final major force that is affecting the time horizon of planners is the expectations of our employees and customers regarding the quality of their lives. We are living in an age in which the demands for the amenities of life are increasing. The people with whom our organizations interact are demanding much more in the way of accommodation to the needs of human existence. Workers are refusing to move at their employers' whim, preferring to change jobs rather than change communities. The Congress, through such vehicles as the new pension law, is supporting this general trend.

The perceived dehumanization of service brought about by computers is being forced back by "ergonomics." To be successful, a product must show that it has been designed for comfortable use.

Even entertainment is not immune to these effects. It appears that people would prefer to stay home and watch television, broadcast or cable, rather than attend an even comparably priced event outside the home. Telebanking, teleshopping, teleworking are all terms representing an accepted task being done at a distance, at home.

The introductory life cycle of these new ways of living appears to be measured in years, not decades.

How does an organization respond when these forces come together all at once? Industries related to the telephone and other, newer modes of communication are being affected by rapid changes in the entertainment environment. Large computers are challenged by small home computers; companies who began by providing word processing equipment are now in the communications and main frame business. As a result of the opportunity offered by new technologies, companies are entering and leaving the marketplace at a rate that almost defies our ability to keep track!

An interesting paradox that arises from these considerations is that the organizations most threatened by the multitude of changes that are occurring are precisely those large enough to employ the staffs capable of doing planning. They are being threatened by small single-product organizations that are "lean and mean." Since they do not have an existing product, they do not have to plan; therefore they are less expensive. The only protection the established organizations have is to plan even harder, making their products even more expensive and their structures more difficult to change to respond to a mortal thrust.

An apparent resolution of this dilemma lies in the ability of the larger organizations to gain parity by establishing a unified planning process, supported by many effective tools, which magnifies the effects of the planners and speeds the introduction of new products. Thus the paradox ought to be resolved and parity introduced. The new organizations cannot afford tools and probably do not need them; the large organizations can afford the tools to create the integrated planning process and will compete effectively only after they are in use.

REFERENCES

1. Black, P., "What Is the Focus of Your Business," *Innovation*, no. 22, 1971.
2. Ansoff, H. I., *Strategic Management*. Wiley, New York, 1979.

QUESTIONS FOR THOUGHT

1. Assume that the executives of your organization decide that they must improve their public image, how would you structure a set of objectives having this end in mind which are actionable, achievable, and measurable?

2. A manufacturer of tools for the home market receives a proposal
    for a major research and development activity in the area of lasers.
    You are the staff assistant to an executive who has been asked to
    look at the alternatives. What would your recommendation be and
    why?

6

Information Systems Strategic Planning: Concepts and Needs

WHAT IS ISSP?

Information systems strategic planning (ISSP) ought to concern itself with the answer to several simple questions. What applications do we need to satisfy our organizational goals? Where shall we place these applications within our organization? Who shall be responsible for their daily operations? What dependencies are implied for these applications, and what do they need to provide the appropriate information to their users?

These questions sound simple, yet the correct answer to them will be very difficult to find. They require an organization to understand its crucial components and the flows of information between organizational structures.

The need to plan has been accepted by most organizations. The scope of the planning process has been extended to include not only tactical plans for the short term but also long-range strategic plans. Planning for information systems should follow the same pattern. However, although most organizations have accepted the need for short-term tactical planning in areas such as capacity planning, it is not universally recognized that some form of strategic planning is also required in the arena of information systems.

Information systems strategic planning refers to the mechanisms by which an organization decides what its long-term goals of information systems delivery will be. For example, an organization may decide that it will shift to an on-line operational environment some time in the next five years. This shift will change the nature of the computational resources it requires to do its work and must be planned for as smoothly as possible. Similarly, an organization may choose to treat data as a corporate resource, much like it treats money as a resource, and because of this conscious choice, its operations must be changed. This too will require a long lead time, and a range of planning periods must be used to insure an effective transition to a different way of doing business.

WHY ISSP IS NEEDED

The examples cited above refer to broad strategic changes in direction. To this must be added the effect of a new information systems environment on the portfolio of applications that an organization needs to survive. Entire categories of applications are introduced when an on-line environment becomes the accepted operational environment. Thus both the provision of the capability and the schedule for the production of the applications have to be tied into the planning process. This combination is very similar to the operational planning environment of most organizations and by analogy, at least, should be treated at the same level of detail.

The effects of a new information systems environment are the primary reason why organizations should consider information systems strategic planning. If the rate of change in the environment is fast enough to force long-range planning, if the increased pace of competition requires the consideration of alternatives, then the pace of technology in a technologically driven area must also require planning. Many of the goods and services of tomorrow will be made possible directly by the enhanced capabilities of technology, and organizations must keep abreast of what is becoming increasingly cost effective in their areas of interest.

An additional reason for requiring long-range planning disciplines in information services is the size of the computational budget in many organizations. It is simply prudent business sense to take into account managed utilization of this costly resource. Even though individual components may be dropping in price the entire data processing budget, consisting of people and machines, is increasing.

For all these reasons it must be understood that the planning disciplines inserted in the last 10 years need to be uniformly applied to the data processing departments. The argument that data processing is akin to research and development and cannot be planned for in a deterministic manner is false. First, research and development is being managed, and second, operational aspects of our organizations depend on data processing resources for their daily work, a dependency that is planned for in as exact a manner as is possible.

EXPLICIT RELATIONSHIP TO BUSINESS STRATEGIC PLANNING

Information systems strategic planning is necessary and is intimately tied to a firm's operations. This relationship implied that the two processes should not be independent of each other. The role of strategic planning, as described above, is to help us set our long-range objectives. Many of these objectives depend on the ability of our information systems group to deliver specific services. To plan for one without the other would be ridiculous. The economies of the developed nations are becoming increasingly service-oriented, with information a vital product and commodity. If the front-line competition is moving to match the degree of service we can provide, to neglect the information systems we depend upon in our strategic planning would be unresponsive and uncompetitive. What is needed is a method that allows us to consider, in a uniform manner, the continuous evolution of our plans in a rapidly changing technology. This methodology would be capable of specifying work in both data processing and business terms. There must be an explicit relationship between business and information systems planning if we are to achieve the benefits of using computers in our organizations.

Linkage to the Desirable

The approach to be followed is one that assumes the rapid pace of technology. In this view we are limited by our ability to imagine the future, not in our ability to achieve it once imagined. An organization's executive officers can all give a description of "heaven" as they imagine it to be. This is a start for the linkage of the two planning environments. In this approach the planning process begins with a long-term projection of the way the organization should operate, in terms of control and for the desired areas of operation. Planners use this as a starting point. What is impossible today will be imaginable tomorrow. What is barely possible today will be reality in a few years. Each area's pace of technological progress is unique and must be tied to what is possible.

Linkage to the Possible

Each impossible dream, when subjected to cold analysis, leads to limiting conditions that must be understood as the linkage to that which is possible in our shorter planning horizons. As technology, including data processing, provides more capability at a better price, we uncover much that can now be done. Understanding the linkage to the possible as a moving target, we create objectives that take into account assumed future capabilities of our support environments. If technology should make an unexpected leap in a particular area, then we would be prepared to jump right in, perhaps gaining a temporary advantage, with already drawn contingency plans. This kind of information is drawn directly from the computer-related disciplines, which therefore must be an integrated part of the planning mechanisms.

Mechanism for Handling Detail

Planning implies keeping track of complexity. Complexity includes the many details associated with the objects and data of our organizations. Computers can keep track of the detail and present it in graphic or report form to aid in the planning process itself. This creates a situation in which information systems capability needs to be bootstrapped across our organizations to be able to use computational capability efficiently. A disciplined methodology must therefore be put into place in all aspects of the planning-related environment, and the methodology and its associated disciplines are then pervasive elements that need to be widely understood.

GENERAL METHODOLOGIES

There are no recipes for successful planning. No one has managed to create a perfect prescription, guaranteed to work, or your money back, for all times, places, and situations. What has become clear, however, is that there are approaches that are sufficiently disciplined to promise some measure of success in most circumstances. These prescriptions are identified as methodologies. The literature abounds with different methodologies and approaches for dealing with the entire gamut of tasks from strategic planning to operational daily planning, for both business planning and information systems planning. The philosophies of some of these methodologies appear mutually contradictory in some instances, and yet it would seem that these apparently contradictory approaches can be made to work together.

The similarity of information systems planning to general business planning becomes more evident when one takes note of the number of high-level systems analysis approaches that have been used for business planning.

When objectives and first causes dominate the methodology, the techniques are quite compatible; when the techniques use jargon and technical details to drive them, they are specialized to one or the other approach.

Methodologies are divided into several groups. There are strong methodologies[1] and weak methodologies. These terms are used to describe the stringency of discipline that the techniques utilize. A strong methodology enforces much discipline in its approach. It constrains the implementer to the greatest possible degree by providing, for example, a language and direction. A weak discipline, on the other hand, does not constrain the designer to the same degree. The designer is freer to choose a language and methods appropriate to the task.

Weak disciplines allow for a greater degree of creativity and hence are applicable in more complex and diverse circumstances; stronger disciplines are applicable in areas of narrower concern. The stronger disciplines are more predictable and controllable, the weaker disciplines less predictable and controllable.

The relationship between these two approaches is complimentary. There are domains in which greater creativity is required for which the weaker methods are more appropriate. The areas where manageability and predictability are more appropriate require the strong methods.

The areas of applicability can also be expressed in terms of problem and solution orientations. Problem-oriented approaches are interested in the nature of the problem, the separation of the disease from the symptoms. The solution-oriented procedures are normally associated with circumstances in which the symptoms must be taken care of first before we have the luxury of dealing with the disease. This translates itself naturally into procedure-oriented approaches and data-structure-oriented approaches. Procedure decomposition begins a spectrum of techniques, from those that, by changing just a little at a time, map out almost every possibility along the way to techniques driven by static data structures.

Procedure Decomposition

The phrase *procedure decomposition* refers to a set of approaches whose major idea is that all problems can be solved by slowly reducing them to more elemental terms. Advocates of procedure decomposition "divide and conquer" each problem as it appears. An early impetus for procedural decomposition was the approach called *stepwise refinement*. The term *refinement* as used here means to grind into ever more finely divided pieces. Since the result of a process of refinement depends to some extent on the places which the divider chooses as break points, each attempt at a solution will invariably lead to a somewhat different result. How good the solution is depends on the skill of the analyst, whose creativity is the necessary talent. This approach is an example of a weak methodology.

Data-Driven Techniques

Data-driven techniques take an approach that is different from the procedure-oriented methodologies. If we are concerned with an issue, the argument goes, we already have a strong opinion about what the world ought to look like. Here, the stimulus that has aroused us is a deviation from some preconceived environment. Data-driven approaches start from the premise of what the preconceived environment will look like and build ways of achieving that state. We begin with the data needed to support the environment and work backwards as a means of arriving there. This is usually a strong approach in the sense of prescribing the way to eliminate the problem. Data-driven approaches tend to be very algorithmic in nature and require more specific training than do the procedure-oriented approaches.

Data-Flow Analysis

The ideas of procedural decomposition and data analysis are both very persuasive. Both seem to contain reasonable attributes for a methodology designed to aid in our controlling an organization's environment. Is there some way of combing attributes from both to provide a synthesis methodology? Data-flow analysis takes as its model the flow of information within an organization. Procedure is viewed as that which assists or directs flow, whereas data is the object, that is flowing. The conceptual strategy that is used is to chart the flows and discover the break points at which natural groupings stem. The data flow is decomposed, and the data structure is derived from a refinement of the flows.

Defining Requirements

It appears that the techniques in use constitute a spectrum of approaches that has strict process decomposition at one end and static data structure on the other. Various combinations of techniques reside in the center of the spectrum. The procedurally oriented mechanisms are typically weaker approaches than the more algorithmically oriented data structure approaches. This generalization seems to hold true in most cases.

It has become customary to describe implementation projects in terms of system or project life cycles. Although it is premature to go through the full discussion of life cycles at this point, it is worthwhile to begin to describe some of the early phases. Such a discussion will enable us to introduce some of the ideas of requirements planning, which are usually part of the early phases of the development process. Many of the recent studies of improving the productivity of software development have pointed to the inability of the data processing profession to determine a complete set of user requirements. In defense of the data processing departments, we must add that users rarely understand their own functions well enough to articulate a set of requirements, or do not understand enough about the capability of the computer as a tool to define a reasonable set of requirements. The purpose of the requirements phase is to ease the transition to an acceptable starting point. To apply this objective to the domain of strategic planning, what we need is an approach that will help us to define an information systems architecture for our organization. There are a group of methodologies which are now being used in information systems strategic planning that either began as requirements procedures for systems or were accepted from the outset as drivers of organizational requirements at the architecture level.

A further differentiation has been pointed out by Davis[2] concerning those approaches that are associated with strategic planning and those that properly belong to the world of computer applications. The higher level is associated with organizational information requirements, the information system's architecture. At this level the portfolio of applications is decided upon and the architecture is established that will be used to describe the general systems structure.

The lower level concentrates on specific applications and generates the specific requirements to be used in the development process. This second level is considered in the next chapter under a single system life cycle. The strategic level is the subject of the subject of the remaining part of this chapter. Examples of specific, practiced techniques will be used to show the divergence of opinion on the proper sequence in which to do strategic systems planning.

SPECIFIC, PRACTICED METHODS

Process Decomposition Type: SADT

SADT,* Structured Analysis and Design Technique,[3] is a methodology developed by SofTech Inc. and used by them in a variety of circumstances and situations. Stemming from a history of difficulties in developing large data processing applications, SADT attacks what appears to be the main cause of confusion: our lack of understanding of the "real" requirements that cause a program to be written. The approach drawn on to ease the difficulty in defining the appropriate requirements is "divide and conquer." The methodology leads the analyst along a path that continuously breaks the problem down, in a patterned manner, from high-level abstraction to concrete terms. "The human mind can accomodate any amont of complexity as long as it is presented in easy-to-grasp chunks that are structured together to make the whole."[4]

In order to provide a useful breakdown of the difficulty at hand, SADT begins by concentrating on why the analyst is called in and attempts to define that context as clearly as possible. This explains why SADT has been found to be useful in planning mechanisms. Discipline combined with a focus on the "why" of the issue at hand provides a blueprint for the planner practicing his or her art. The approach attempts to draw upon some of the aspects of behavioral psychology and learning theory to make the technique easy to use and to enable people to make the complexity of the process more manageable.

Contextual Analysis. SADT attempts to bypass the concerns often raised about curing the symptoms rather than the disease by forcing planners to concentrate on the "why" of the process rather than on the "what" that can eliminate pain. It is recognized that of the many valid points of view that can be used to express the current condition, SADT

---

*Trademark of SofTech, Inc.

concentrates on three during context analysis: technical assessment, operational assessment, and economic assessment.

The relationship between these three areas is shown pictorially in Figure 6.1. The systems analyst or planner must be able to read through the diagram and put into words the relationships identified. The narrative that results from the successful navigation of the table would read as follows: The current operations of our organization are . . . , and this has caused a problem whose symptoms are . . . . Our organization is sensitive to these symptoms because . . . . If we supply these proposed functions operating in our environment with these performance characteristics, then the effect on our organization will be *a, b, c,* . . . . The resources required to deliver the function proposed will operate under these conditions and will cost a specified number of dollars.

If a systems analyst or planner is capable of completing this prescription, then the organization is well on its way toward understanding the *why* of its effort. This kind of thinking leads to three assessments of the planning process: technical, operational, and financial. Although each of these views is valid, all too often only one is expressed during planning; because each of these views tends to be advanced by a particular specialist, the result is a concentration on the trees rather than the forest.

Technical Imperative. The technical issues arise when reading down the columns vertically and are driven by an understanding of current operations and what functions and resources can be implemented to

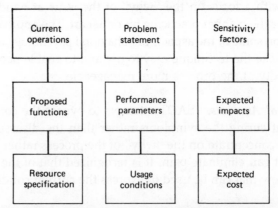

Figure 6.1. Multiple viewpoints of requirements definition.

improve these current operations. This describes the view of the technician, which tends to lead to a solution that delivers more of the same but presumably at a higher level of efficiency.

Operational Viability. Operations are sensitive to symptoms. Reading the middle columns downwards produces a solution to eliminate pain. The solution concentrates on how we ought to behave to eliminate the problem. Again a specialist has avoided looking toward the first cause, the *why* of the current level of pain. The combination of the two points of view leads us to at least a feasible solution within the constraints of technology. The third view is needed to finally tie together these three points of view into a coherent planning process.

Economic Sensitivity. The sensitivity of the organization to the symptoms already felt determine how deeply we must dig to find the root cause of the disease. With enough sensitivity we must dig down to the foundations; with little sensitivity we can afford to just treat the symptoms. The combination of all three views makes possible the synergy that SADT hopes to unveil by a controlled methodology.

Conceptual Modeling. The analysis is continued in the same manner by moving through a patterned set of "what," "why," and "how" questions addressed to the completed table. This table represents the beginning of a conceptual model of the objectives of the organization and of how we proceed to implement them. At each step we end with a "how" question, and the "how" is answered by further subdividing our understanding into more pieces, each of which is further analysed in the same pattern.

The SADT rule of thumb is that all items identified at the current level should be further subdivided into no fewer than three nor more than six pieces. This is the procedural decomposition method, which categorizes it in the framework used here. The process continues until a sufficient level of detail is reached for the analysing group. The direction is from the top down, initiated by a strong search for fundamental objectives to begin the process. The three questions help to define how each of the items are bound within their contexts. "What" represents the constraints of what is to be delivered; "why" represents the conditions that require these items to be delivered; "how" represents the implementation to be used to produce the items to be delivered.

Data and Activity.   Organizations and systems both depend on two assets. One is the procedures or activities that experience has shown to be valuable and the other, data, the numbers which describe an organization. The SADT approach recognizes the importance of both of these and views them as duals of each other. They are the opposite sides of the same coin, and when one is handled, its counterpart must also be handled.

SADT points to such other dual elements as analogues, nouns and verbs, objects and operations, passive and active, and data and activities. The specification of both leads to the functional architecture of the system (strategy) being specified.

Graphical Display.   A major component of the SADT methodology is the graphical display used to deliver the information developed. It is the belief of the authors that the form of the documentation is extremely important if it is to be read and understood. An analogy is drawn to the engineering professions where blueprints are a universal language. The standard symbols used are understood by all levels of that profession, and each time they are studied, even by the most junior member, a mental simulation of the model represented by the blueprint is carried out. Is it any wonder that so few buildings collapse compared to strategic plans and systems which are adequate for their needs? SADT attempts to fill this gap by defining a graphical language to communicate ideas based on well-understood symbols.

The unit of representation for the ideas is the box with arrows entering or leaving from all sides. In an activity diagram the boxes represent activities, and the arrows, data flows; in a data diagram the roles are reversed. A descriptive example of such boxes with the meanings of the arrows is shown in Figure 6.2 and Figure 6.3.

In an activity diagram the arrows represent data flows and the name inside the box is an activity. As one would suppose, arrows entering from the right represent input data, and arrows exiting to the left are output data. The activity transforms the input into the desired product of that transformation. An arrow that enters from the top represents control information. For example, if a budget, by constraining the number of dollars to be spent, controls the level of the transformation, it would enter pictorially from the top. Arrows entering from the bottom represent mechanisms that support the current activity, the databases

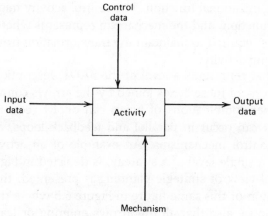

Figure 6.2 SADT activity box.

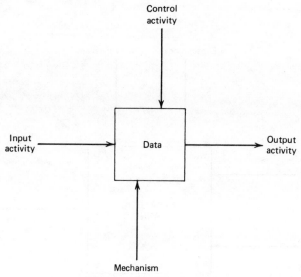

Figure 6.3 SADT data box.

of standards or reference materials that are used in carrying out the current activity.

The data diagrams are defined in a parallel manner. The contents of the box represent a named data store or file and the right and left side arrows represent the activities used to generate that data and that use it in some organizational function. The control activity might represent a standards function, and the mechanism represents whatever updates the references required to maintain the transformation from generating activity to using activity.

An item that represents a level of the SADT description consists of from three to six of these boxes joined by the arrows connecting them. In this manner combinations of boxes can depict sequential activity, activities that can occur in parallel and feedback loops, and any of a number of control mechanisms. An example of an activity diagram, representing a single level of a strategy, is depicted in Figure 6.4.

A top-level view of strategic planning is presented, then amplified in the explosion of this same figure in Figure 6.5 where the rule of 3–6 is obeyed. Notice also that all the arrows entering or leaving *strategic planning* also enter and leave boxes in the level-1 diagram, with the number of off-page connectors remaining the same. This does not imply

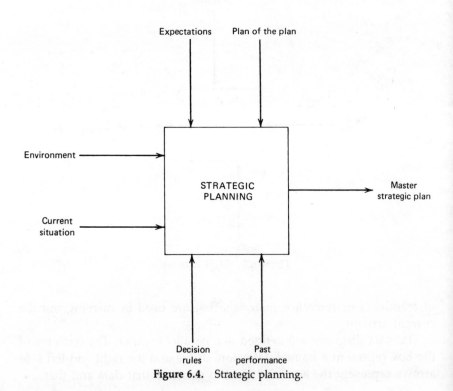

Figure 6.4. Strategic planning.

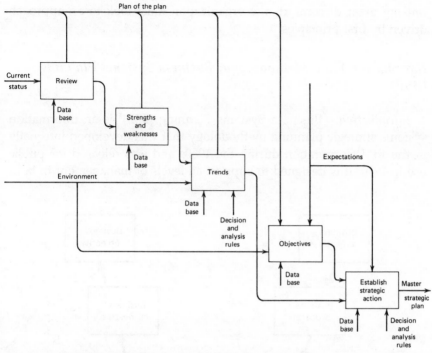

Figure 6.5. Strategic planning expanded.

that inputs must enter the first box and outputs leave from the last, which may in fact occur at any of the boxes on the page.

Domain of Applicability. SADT was created to be a tool of analysis that could be used in determining what an organization's requirements are for a data processing application. It concentrates on the primary pitfall of arriving at a proper solution to the wrong problem. To achieve these goals it has to stretch for the primary objectives each application must satisfy to attain the organization's goals. This stretching back to first causes makes SADT a good, high-level planning approach. The primary objectives of the organization need to be articulated and documented so that they can evolve into effective tactical plans. The decompositions that stem from the high-level diagrams channel the thinking of the planners into "actionable" approaches. If the basic objectives have already been documented and if a particular symptom is causing great discomfort, the organization must look to an approach driven by first principles.

Information Flow Methodology: Business Systems Planning (BSP)

Introduction. Business Systems Planning (BSP)[5] is an information systems strategic planning methodology that was developed internally in the IBM Corporation during the 1960s and was released for public use in 1970. It is designed to support all levels of management in both

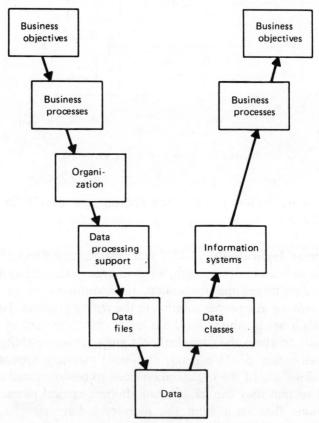

Figure 6.6. Top-down, bottom-up aspects of BSP study. *(Reprinted by permission of IBM Corp.)*

short- and long-term planning in a way that meshes with an organization's overall business plan.

BSP is a data-oriented methodology that is driven by the flow of data and resources through an organization. Since it recognizes that an efficient information system must be based on the intelligent organization and use of the firm's data, it relies on the emerging concept of managing data as a resource. The intent in BSP is to analyze a business organization in a top-down fashion, from a high-level view. By studying the various business processes that a firm performs to meet its ultimate objectives, a framework of the data needed by those processes can be built. Furthermore, an understanding of the flow of data from one part of a business to another can be derived. A sense of the underlying data requirements and data flows, at a high level of detail, forms the common base from which to proceed further with implementation of the information systems. While BSP provides a top-down analysis of a business, its common, data-oriented base understanding of the business is intended to provide a foundation for a modular, bottom-up style of implementation of the information systems. The decision about which piece to implement first is made on a priority basis, but can be made independent of the other parts. Figure 6.6 shows the essence of the top-down analysis, bottom-up implementation approach. Notice that the result of the analysis and the starting point for implementation are data.

Methodology. Figure 6.7 presents an outline of the BSP methodology. In describing each step of the figure, we will shed more light on the BSP philosophy.

Gaining the Commitment. At the outset, the set of personnel involved must be established. For such an effort to work, it must have the sponsorship of a high-level executive. The study team should consist of about four to seven employees. They should, if possible, be middle or upper management people who have a solid understanding of their part of the business, as well as a good background in the workings of the rest of the organization. They should expect to spend six to eight weeks of full-time work on the study.

The sponsor must set the scope of the study. Depending on the size of the organization and the information systems needs, it might encom-

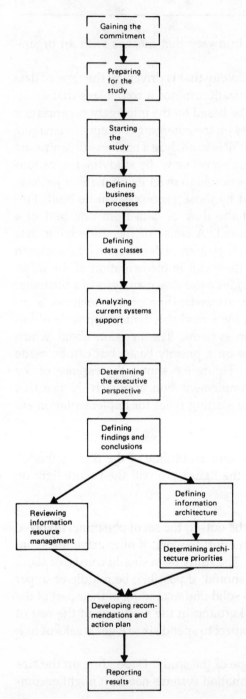

Figure 6.7. Flow of the BSP study.
(Reprinted by permission of IBM Corp.)

pass the entire company, a group of divisions, or a single division. The precise objectives and a business case justification of the study must be developed. Finally, all of that information must be presented to the organization's top management for approval.

Preparing for and Starting the Study. The study team should map out its plan of attack, which should include an understanding of the information about the business and about the existing information systems that must be gathered as input. It also involves a list of the sources from whom the information can be gotten. Appropriate information about the business would involve: environment, objectives, organization, planning, measurement and control, operations, and information systems support. As for the information systems, the data should include a list of existing systems, systems under development, and systems being planned, as well as a general understanding of the processing mode and size of the environment.

Another important function at this stage is to establish a series of control points to review the progress of the study.

Defining Business Processes. BSP defines business processes as "groups of logically related decisions and activities required to manage the resources of the business." The processes must be defined in such a way as to make them independent of changes in management structures based on whim rather than need or other good cause.

There are three types of processes: planning and control processes, product/service processes, and supporting resources processes. The category of planning and control processes consists of two parts: strategic planning processes, such as economic forecasting and organization planning, and management control processes such as market forecasting and budgeting. Product/service processes involve the operations directly related to the generation of the firm's revenues. Supporting resource processes are those that involve such resources as materials, money, facilities, and personnel.

For the categories of product/service and supporting resource processes, the following method is used to discern the actual business processes. Take each product/service and supporting resource and follow them through their life cycle. The four stages in the life cycle are: (1) requirements, planning, measurement, and control, (2) acquisition or implementation, (3) stewardship, and (4) retirement or disposition.

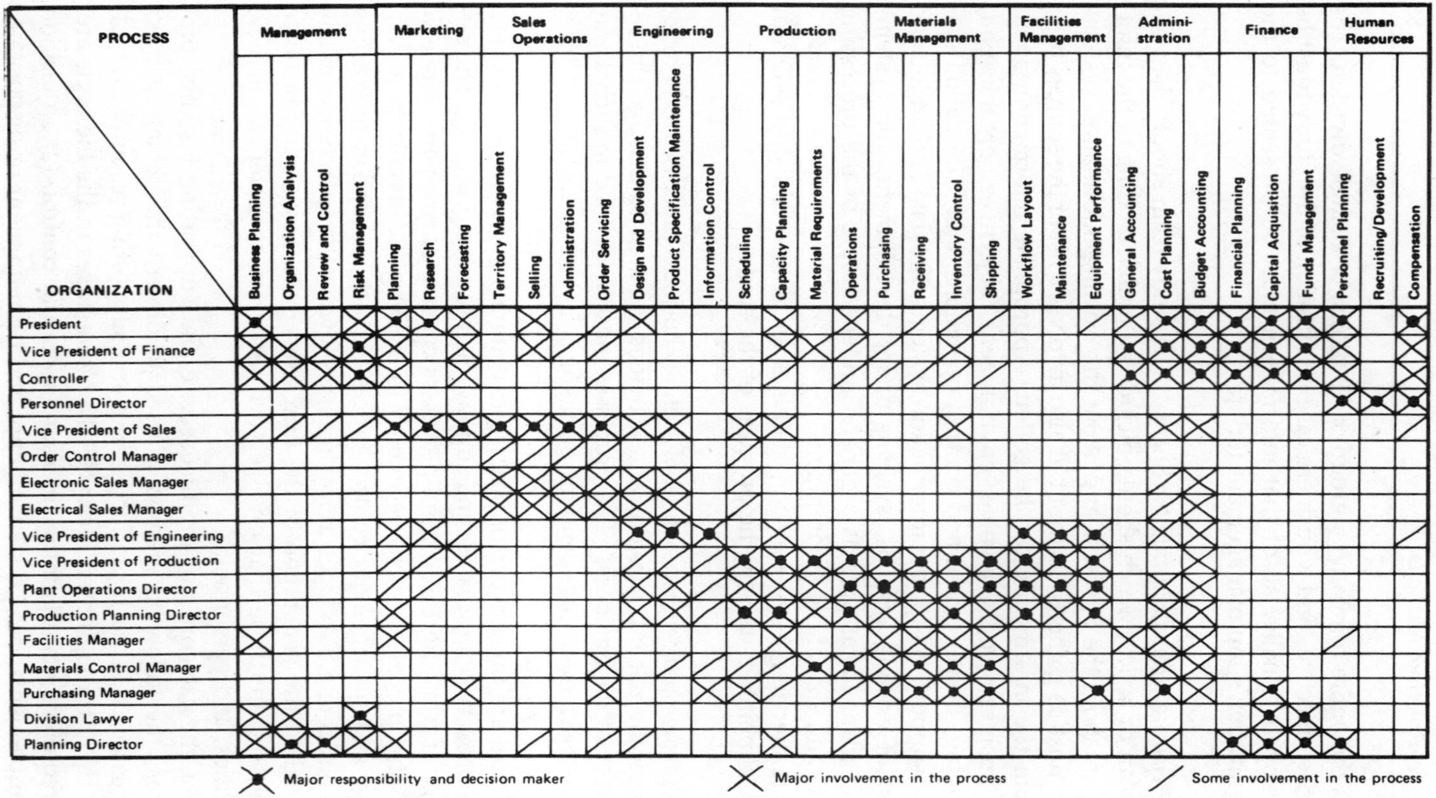

Figure 6.8. Process/organization matrix. (*Reprinted by permission of IBM Corp.*)

☒ Major responsibility and decision maker   ╳ Major involvement in the process   ╱ Some involvement in the process

The processes that are necessary to handle the product/service or supporting resource in each stage are the pertinent processes for the BSP study.

The list of discovered processes must then be refined. Processes involving widely differing levels of detail must be resolved. In some cases processes may be combined or a process split into several parts. It will be helpful to organize the processes into groups, such as finance and sales management. There should be 4 to 12 groups and no more than 60 total processes. Finally, a matrix, Figure 6.8, is drawn indicating which executives or organizations have which of three levels of responsibility or involvement (if any) in which processes.

Defining Data Classes. A data class is "a category of logically related data that is necessary to support the business." Ultimately, it will be seen that a data class is a set of closely related data fields, but at this point the concern is with broader categories of data.

To determine the 30 to 60 data classes that one should expect to find, an analysis can be made that loosely follows the life cycle form for processes. The four basic types of data classes are: (1) inventory data, which relate to the stewardship of a resource, (2) transaction data, which involve events, conversion of resources, or transfer of resources, (3) plans/models data, such as forecasts, budgets, and so on, and (4) statistical/summary data, including transaction summaries and histories.

Once the data classes have been determined, they must be related to the processes in a matrix. That matrix, Figure 6.9, will indicate which processes create the data in which data classes, and, in addition, which processes use data in data classes that they do not create. The processes are arranged in life-cycle order from top to bottom, and the data classes are arranged in a corresponding manner, such that the "create" boxes form a rough diagonal from upper left to lower right.

Analyzing Current Systems Support. At this point, several matrices are created to confirm the understanding of the current state of information systems organization. Many of the future information systems developments that derive from the BSP study must face the reality of having to migrate from the current systems. After making a list of the existing data processing applications, one should create two matrices: one that relates the systems to the executives/areas of the business that

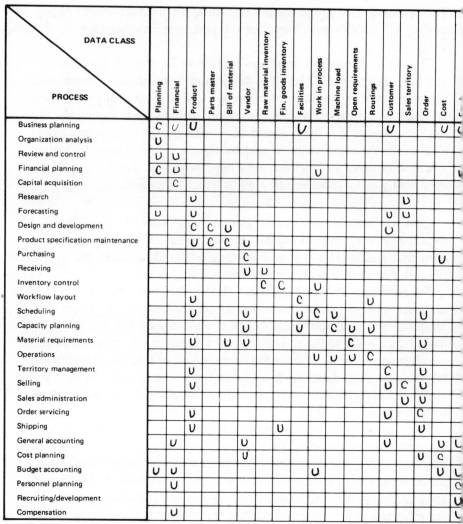

Figure 6.9. Data classes arranged by creating process. *(Reprinted by permission of IBM Corp.)*

they support, and one that relates the systems to the business process that they support. Those two matrices will lead to a more detailed organization versus process matrix, showing which systems support which executives as they are involved in which processes (Figure 6.10). Finally, a matrix should be created to show which systems use which data classes.

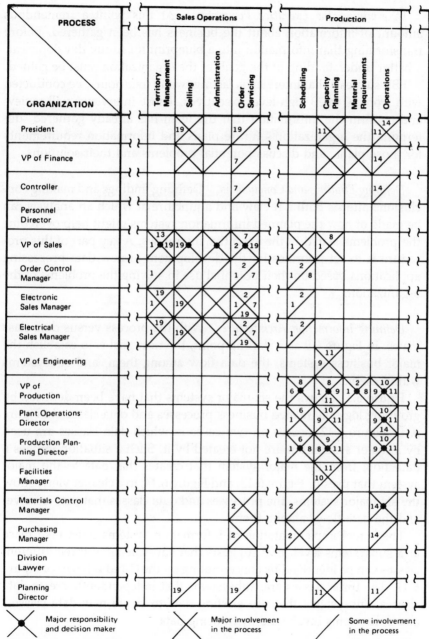

Figure 6.10. Process/organization/current system matrix. (*Reprinted by permission of IBM Corp.*)

Determining the Executive Perspective. At this point a tremendous amount of information about the business has been gathered. Before transforming that information into a blueprint for future development, a better understanding of the goals of the organization must be gained.

BSP suggests that interviews, lasting two to four hours, be conducted with from 10 to 20 high-level executives. Those interviews will review and confirm the information that the team has already gathered, determine the organization's future plans and information requirements for those plans, and discuss potential problems and their solutions.

Defining Findings and Conclusions. Defining findings and making conclusions affords both a review and a juncture at which an analysis can be made of how the planned information systems might help overcome the problems stated in the executive interviews. A key part of this procedure is to set priorities for the development of new data processing applications based on their potential use in solving the problems of the organization.

Defining Information Architecture. With the process versus data class matrix in Figure 6.9 as a starting point, the next goal is to establish the major business systems, the data flow among them, and subsystems within them.

Figure 6.11 shows the six major systems that have been deduced by grouping logically related business processes and data classes in Figure 6.10. Figure 6.12 focuses on two cases in which data classes are used by a major system but are not created by it. Such a situation implies a data flow from the major system that creates that data to the major system that uses it. Figure 6.13, and Figure 6.14, in a cleaner view, show the six major systems, the processes and data classes that they involve, and the data flows among them.

The actual implementation of information systems must take place at a subsystems level. BSP suggests that subsystems of three different classes can be identified by concentrating on the *C* and *U* boxes of Figure 6.11. The three classes are: subsystems that independently create data classes, subsystems that use existing data to create new data classes, and subsystems involved only in using data.

Determining Architecture Priorities. Once the major systems and the subsystems have been established, the order of implementation remains

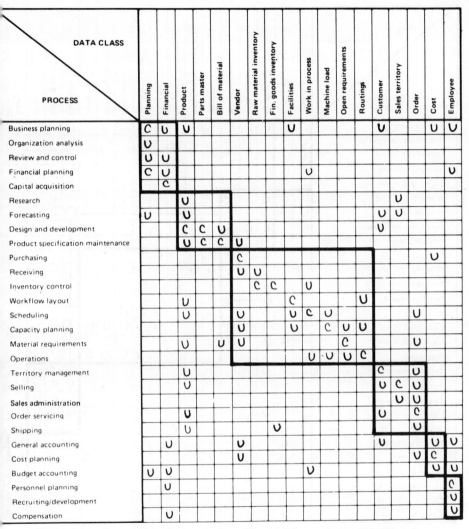

PROCESS \ DATA CLASS	Planning	Financial	Product	Parts master	Bill of material	Vendor	Raw material inventory	Fin. goods inventory	Facilities	Work in process	Machine load	Open requirements	Routings	Customer	Sales territory	Order	Cost	Employee
Business planning	C	U	U						U					U			U	U
Organization analysis	U																	
Review and control	U	U																
Financial planning	C	U								U								U
Capital acquisition		C																
Research			U												U			
Forecasting	U		U											U	U			
Design and development			C	C	U									U				
Product specification maintenance			U	C	C	U												
Purchasing						C											U	
Receiving						U	U											
Inventory control							C	C		U								
Workflow layout			U						C				U					
Scheduling			U							U	C	U				U		
Capacity planning									U	U	C	U	U					
Material requirements			U		U		U					C				U		
Operations										U	U	U	C					
Territory management			U											C		U		
Selling			U											U	C	U		
Sales administration														U	C			
Order servicing			U											U		C		
Shipping			U					U								U		
General accounting		U				U								U			U	U
Cost planning						U								U			C	
Budget accounting	U	U							U								U	U
Personnel planning		U																C
Recruiting/development																		U
Compensation		U																U

Figure 6.11. Process/data class groupings. *(Reprinted by permission of IBM Corp.)*

to be decided. The bottom-up order of implementation of the subsystems will be based on system benefits, impact on the business, probability of success, and demand. Appropriate documentation for these and other issues of the subsystems should be generated.

Reviewing Information Resource Management. The point is made that, in parallel with the information architecture work, the study team

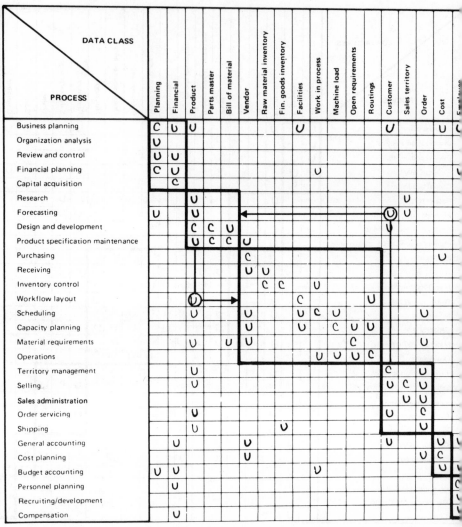

Figure 6.12. Data flow determination. *(Reprinted by permission of IBM Corp.)*

should be reviewing and making recommendations on the organization's approach to information resource management. The systems oriented information architecture cannot succeed without a well-developed and well-managed approach to managing the organization's data.

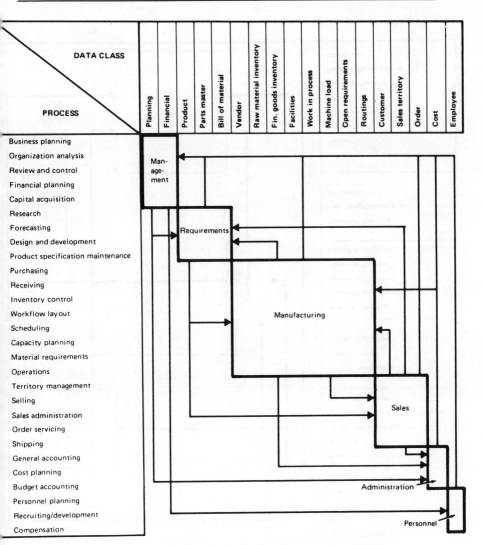

Figure 6.13. Information architecture. *(Reprinted by permission of IBM Corp.)*

Developing Recommendations and Action Plan and Reporting Results. Finally, the study team must organize all of the work that it has done and present it to management for approval. The report and presentation will include the information architecture and recommendations for subsystem implementation. Each recommendation should include

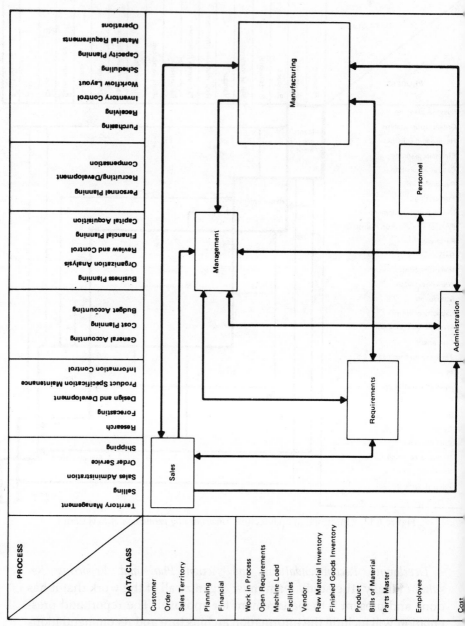

Figure 6.14. Graphic rearrangement of information architecture. *(Reprinted by permission of IBM Corp.)*

a cost-benefit analysis and an indication of how it will help the organization.

Static Structure Methodologies: BIAIT

Are companies and organizations different from each other, with independent data processing needs, or are there commonalities that could allow the analyst to identify generic business functions? BIAIT (Business Information Analysis and Integration Technique), derived from the research of Donald C. Burnstine,[6] answers that question affirmatively. Burnstine checked 300 or 400 different business-related questions and came to the conclusion that there exists only 7 independent questions that distinguish between the ways an organization can use information. These questions apply to the basic trigger of all businesses, the order.

As Burnstine saw it, an order is a general system component that has the effect of either requesting or forcing a flow of information. Orders may be for material things such as finished goods or raw materials. They may be issued to reserve a space, such as an airplane seat, or to obtain a skill through any means, from education to the hiring of a construction worker. The order is the trigger that causes the other parts of the organization to respond. The range of responses, however, is constrained and can be specified by the "yes" or "no" answer to the seven questions regarding business variables (Figure 6.15).

Order states. The first business variable is whether the customer gets billed or pays for the product directly. The answer to this question tells the analyst which information-handling disciplines (IHD) must be present in this organization. A "yes" answer to the previous questions suggests that a billing discipline must be in force. The second question is associated with whether the product is delivered later or the customer buys it and takes it home. If the first option is true, we know that an order entry/tracking system must be in place.

In some businesses a complete customer profile is kept, whereas in others it is not necessary. This difference has implications for record keeping and analysis. Some prices are negotiated; others are fixed. Some products are rented; others are purchase; and still others can be in both states for different customers. The IHDs required to control each and

YES	VARIABLE	NO
The supplier bills the consumer.	BILL	The order is paid for with cash or a cash equivalent (check or charge card).
The supplier maintains information about the consumer order until the order is satisfied.	FUTURE	The consumer takes what is ordered with him.
The supplier keeps records by individual customer about price transactions (for purposes other than billing).	PROFILE	The supplier does not keep records about prior transactions with individual customers (every customer is a surprise).
The consumer and supplier negotiate price.	NEGOTIATE	The transaction is fixed price (to any given set of customers).
The supplier rents the product to the consumer; the supplier retains title.	RENT	The consumer buys the product and takes title to it.
The supplier keeps track of the product for subsequent recall or change.	TRACK	The supplier does not track the product.
The product is made to the consumer's specifications, or assembled from an existing specification.	MADE TO ORDER	The product is provided from stock (no processing performed to produce the product).

Figure 6.15. Business Variables.

specified in a master model are known to the analyst when he determines the answer to the question related to the business variable of *rent*.

The last two variables are whether or not the product is tracked for potential recall, as in the automobile industry, and whether a product is built to the customer's specification or comes from stock. The sequence of the questions shows the complexity of the IHDs required to support a "yes" answer. The later in the list the "yes" occurs, the more complex the support needs to be.

The seven questions give rise to 128 independent organizational types, which define a generic model that can be used to describe the gross IHD support that an organization requires. The analysis required to reach this level of understanding is simple, and the time to completion is measured in hours. This gives the analyst and his client a common vocabulary for discussion. It is also related to the idea of the critical success factors of Rockart. The approach quickly identifies what is on the executive's mind.

The Role of Data. Burnstine mapped the system life cycle onto a functional view of the organization and for each of the IHD procedures identified by the business variable choices identified the flow of data in terms of responsibility and use. Each of the IHDs is responsible for keeping track of a data inventory. Kerner, who extended BIAIT named 12 of these data inventories (Figure 6.16). The first column of Figure 6.16 is reminiscent of Forestor's[7] resources, while the second identifies relationships among the resources specified in the first column.

Each of the data inventories is divided into two types of information: planning and actual information. The planning and actual information, used for the management and control of the organization, take further forms of descriptive and value information. In Kerner's formulation, each of the data inventories has some number of data classes associated with its description, which are mapped against organization and problems/measures to determine basic concerns. Kerner identified 23 order-independent data classes and 35 order-dependent data classes, listed in the Appendix of his article.

Clearly the approach is driven by the idea that there exists some small number of organizational models, and an even smaller number of IHDs. The role of the analyst is to first determine the general group to which this business belongs and then to do the small amount of tailoring required to bring this analysis into very sharp focus. The first phase is measured in hours and the second in weeks.

Product	Activity
Customer	Incoming order
Vendor	Track
Facilities	Product description
Employee	Process description
Money	Outgoing order

Figure 6.16. Data inventories.

Domain of Applicability. BIAIT and the related technique of BICS,[8] Business Information Control Study methodology, are still new, and their generic applicability is still being looked at. BICS[9] is attempting to marry some of the approaches of BSP to BIAIT and to store the known analysis in some type of automated model so that an early business model can be constructed. It would appear that in those instances where the way an organization processes its information is significantly different from the way in which other similar organizations process their information, the analysts need to take a very close look. This is certainly a new insight into comparative operations. If an organization understands its business very well, these techniques give a useful checklist of what needs to be done and what ought to be controlled better.

When an organization is having difficulty in articulating its basic objectives, it must first identify its problem at that level and SADT and BSP appear to be better choices as information systems planing tools in that case.

REFERENCES

1. Ramsey, H. R., Atwood, M. E., and Campbell, G. D., "An Analysis of Software Design Methodologies," U.S. Army Research Institute for the Behavioral and Social Sciences, Technical Report 401, Alexandria, VA, 1979.

2. Davis, G. B., "Strategies for Information Requirements Definition," *IBM Systems Journal*, vol. 21, no. 1, 1982, pp. 24–30.

3. Ross, Douglas T., "Structured Analysis (SA): A Language for Communicating Ideas," *IEEE Transactions on Software Engineering*, vol. SE-3, no. 1, 1977.

4. Ross, Douglas T., and Schoman, Kenneth E., Jr., "Structured Analysis for Requirements Definition," *IEEE Transactions on Software Engineering*, vol. SE-3, no. 1 1977.

5. *Business Systems Planning—Information Systems Planning Guide* GE20-0527-3, 3rd ed., IBM Corp., White Plains, NY, 1981.

6. Burnstine, D. C., and Soknacki, D. W., "BIAIT—A Tool for Deciding between Doing the Right Thing and Doing the 'Thing' Right," Application Development Symposium, October 14–17, 1979, GUIDE International, SHARE Inc., IBM.

7. Forrester, Jay W. *Industrial Dynamics*, MIT Press, Cambridge, MA, 1961.

8. Kerner, D. V., "Business Information Control Study Methodology," in R. Goldberg and H. Lorin (eds.), *The Economics of Information Processing*, vol. 1, Wiley, New York, 1982.

9. Zachman, J. A., "Business Systems Planning and Business Information Control Study: A Comparison," *IBM Systems Journal*, vol 21, no. 1, 1982.

QUESTIONS FOR THOUGHT

1. For each of the following situations decide whether a weak or strong planning methodology would be more appropriate.

   a. Improving market share in a mature industry.

   b. Responding to a strategic ballistic missile threat.

   c. Improving customer relations.

2. Describe the steps that might be associated with adding a feature to an already existing product by using the SADT approach. Do the analysis for at least three levels of the hierarchy.

3. It has been said that a business which cannot verbalize its objectives so that each executive understands its intent is in mortal peril. Using BSP as the analysis methodology, show where this confusion might be identified and why it would make completion of a BSP study very difficult.

4. Using BIAIT as the analysis method, compare the information transmission businesses of the Postal Service, The Telephone Company, Western Union, and a package delivery service.

7

Detailed Systems Analysis: Background

The production of programs and systems that can satisfy an organization's need for data processing support can be a very complex matter. The strategic planning outlined in the previous chapters leads us to that point when a particular set of applications has to be chosen and specified in detail, and the process of creation begun. A successful implementation will have to take into account detail because it is the small things that spell the difference between a satisfied user of data processing and a frustrated user.

The meaning of systems analysis changes, depending on whether it is spelled with a capital S or a small s. When the purpose of the professional is to analyze a system and understand its components and directions at a high level, then it is spelled with a capital S. Strategic planning and Systems Analysis are closely related at this level.

When the job to be done is understanding how a particular organizational need is to be satisfied, exactly how a business process works, then systems analysis is a discipline of details.

ROLE OF THE SYSTEMS ANALYST

The systems analyst must be able to understand the disciplines of data processing and the disciplines of the organization's business. The relationship between these two areas and the current level of technology determine the intersection between what is feasible and what is desirable. Each potential application must be subjected to a series of examinations to determine whether the function requested will in fact result in the quality of performance that has been asked for by the user. If that improvement seems to be feasible and the resources required to build the application are available, the project is given a green light to proceed. At this juncture the role of the systems analyst changes, and the detail indicated earlier must now be spelled out. This is accomplished by identifying the functions that will be delivered when the application is complete. These will represent the "tests" that the completed application must satisfy to prove that the requirements have indeed been met.

When the detail has been established and the "what" fully specified, at least in its first version, the role of the systems analyst, changing one more time, now shifts to software architect and project manager. The "what" must be translated into a "how," together with a continuous

102

verification that the application continues to satisfy the detailed systems specifications.

The job functions included within the title *systems analyst* and the profession of systems analysis are thus seen to be extremely broad. Many organizations define a category called *programmer/analyst*, broadening the description even further. Individuals and organizations thus fall into a wide spectrum of usage as far as this title is concerned. The largest have separate analysis and programming departments, with analysts "living" either with a data processing group or with the business organization that will use the application. Some organizations have a job title of *systems architect*, some *project manager*, and some *systems designer*. We will use a definition that talks about the function and not the people filling the roles. Systems analysis will be discussed in terms of these functions from early definition up to but not including the actual writing of code.

WHAT DOES SYSTEMS ANALYSIS DO?

Detailed systems analysis works backwards compared to other ways of analyzing problems. An analyst is called in and is given a solution with the task of designing a system that will produce the results described. The details that need to be filled in include understanding the sources and types of data required, and the procedures that must be put into place to manage the timely and correct delivery and transformation of that data. An application is an organization function in which people make judgements because of the timely availability of data. It may occupy many discrete steps, and, in a particular computer implementation, a series of programs. If the system involves programs that execute in a batch mode, then there is considerable time between steps. When the programs execute in an on-line mode, the immediacy of the judgements and the effects of data input are more crucial. In either instance the job of systems analysis breaks into two distinct activities.

First, the data needed to support the application must be understood. The sequence of operations that chain backwards from the desired outputs to the source of data must be analyzed in terms of definition, form, and location of storage. If a piece of data is not already been captured, then the data standardization process of the organization (whatever that may be) must be followed. This part of the systems analysis process is depicted in Figure 7.1.

The second major component of systems analysis is the set of procedures that must be put into place to capture the data and supply direction to the processing when human judgement is a part of the logical design of the system. This element is much more crucial when we are dealing with an on-line application. Each of the steps that must be carried out needs to be sequenced and understood. The ease with which the people who are partners in the operation of any system interact with that system determines its eventual success or failure. The two components in this process are described in Figure 7.2.

The first component looks at the operating cycles of the organization to determine in what order the data, already specified in the previous step, ought to be processed. These system cycles represent the work order and sequence of programs that the data processing production function is concerned with. These cycles are also dependent on the availability of the appropriate information to generate the next transformation required by the normal work sequence.

The concern, raised more and more frequently, that these steps fit

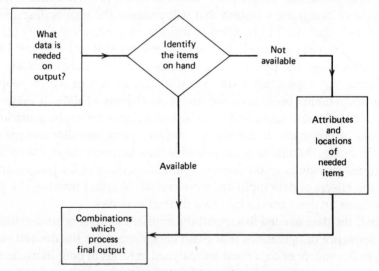

Figure 7.1. Data analysis phase of systems analysis.

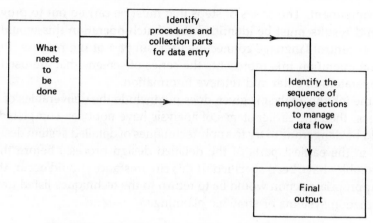

Figure 7.2. Procedure analysis phase of systems analysis.

the human factors requirements of ease of use and satisfaction are also addressed at this time. The sequence of steps that need to be performed has to be set up in such a way that the flows that are created interface well with human operators. For on-line applications this step concerns itself with the sequence of video display screens used and the placement of the data on these screens.

A new approach to the design of application systems involves the creation of prototypes[1] that provide at least a mock-up of the external function that the system is to deliver. These prototypes furnish a means of comparing the effects and operations that the human operators experience, giving them an early chance to notice problems and comment on the ease of use of these systems. If all the screens are available as products of systems analysis, then a tight feedback loop is established early in the development process, which improves the chances that whatever is built represents the solution to a real "ergonomic" problem.

In this description of systems analysis, the focus has been on the inputs and outputs of the process. The inputs were described as being the assignment given at the beginning of analysis and the outputs were described as being the result of two different operations. Data, the subject of the first operation, represents the raw information required by the organization, and systems analysis concentrates on it and its appropriate definition and standardization. Process represents the other key component. The series of steps that must be carried out to provide the end results must be identified. In a batch operation this would be the job control language connecting each subpart of the process. In an on-line operation this represents the series of screens that are used by the operators to enter and retrieve information.

If the job the analyst is given does not include the deliverables of the process, then the earlier stages of analysis have not been completed. It would be dangerous to try to apply techniques of detailed system design, even in the earliest parts of the detailed design process, before these deliverables have been specified. If this circumstance should occur, then the appropriate action would be to return to the techniques listed under information systems or strategic planning.

THE APPLICATION DEVELOPMENT CYCLE

The set of steps that an organization goes through to produce a workable application is called the *application development cycle*. It is important that the steps that each organization passes through remain reasonably constant from application to application. The names of each of the steps are not universally accepted, and even the boundaries between steps keep shifting. A recent phenomenon has been to call for a reexamination of even the general nature of these steps. One thing remains clear, however: Large applications, using considerable scarce resources, with stringent hardware requirements, need to be tightly managed. Smaller applications or those that relax the resource constraints need not be managed as tightly. A typical list of the steps included in the application development process is described by members of Touche Ross & Co.[2] and is given in Table 7.1. A slightly different view of the same process appeared in the literature of a recent conference. The call for papers, which was sent out among professionals, used a prototypical list of the application development life-cycle steps[3] (see Table 7.2). Although the names of the major steps do not seem to be the same as those used by Touche Ross and Co., the descriptions certainly include similar material. As indicated previously the boundaries and descriptions are different, which makes comparisons by the casual reader very frustrating. If the reader examines the descriptions of each closely, the material does over-

Table 7.1   Application Development Phases According to Touche Ross & Co.

Phase I Systems Planning
  Initial investigation
  Feasibility study
Phase II Systems Requirements
  Operations and systems analysis
  User requirements
  Technical support approach
  Conceptual design and package review
  Alternatives evaluation and development planning
Phase III Systems Development
  Systems technical specification
  Technical support development
  Application specifications
  Application programming and testing
  User procedures and controls
  User training
  Implementation planning
  Conversion planning
  Systems test
Phase IV Systems Implementation
  Conversion and phased implementation
  Refinement and tuning
  Postimplementation review
Systems Maintenance
  Ongoing maintenance

Table 7.2   Application Development Phases.

Organizational Analysis
Systems Evaluation
Feasibility Analysis
Project Plan
Logical Design
Physical Design
Program Design
Implementation
Operation
Review and Evaluation

lap, leading to what appears to be an exhaustive coverage of project management.

If the entire sequence of steps, which seems to be quite imposing, were required for every system produced, then problems in the management of systems development would come as no surprise. But in fact the full set of steps is recommended only in the most complex cases. When we are dealing with a relatively simple application, then the items listed are simply road markers waved at in passing or paused at for a view of the scenery. A category of computer applications, transactional processing systems, like reservation systems, are being integrated into the daily activities of companies. These systems will be around for decades and are extremely complex. Their performance is always resource constrained. Informational programs are written to answer specific questions that are important now but will probably not be executed on a periodic basis. Because they are usually not resource constrained, they require less-rigorous management techniques.

The initial steps in systems planning (Table 7.1) and the organizational analysis and system evaluation described in Table 7.2 both concern high-level planning tasks. They involve organizational wide activities such as product selection and organizational structure and are part of information systems strategic planning. The operation we are examining in this chapter begins with feasibility analysis and ends with logical design. In feasibility analysis, a first description of the deliverables, the outputs of systems analysis, is followed by an economic justification for the project. Once successfully justified, a project plan is formalized and the specifications required for implementation are produced. The act of construction and the disciplines that enter the coding and testing of systems are outside the domain of this book, but certain aspects of operation, review, and evaluation need to be stressed.

Management Control

The track record of data processing has not been good when we consider the number of projects that have gotten out of control. The idea of an application development cycle has merit even if we do not agree with each of the phases and their definitions. There has been so much disagreement on the names that in all probability none of the proponents of a particular sequence is totally correct. The more important point is that giving a name to a phase and describing the corresponding process allow management to discuss technical areas in a controlled manner. The discipline that an official approach engenders becomes useful when application development technologies change, when hardware technologies change, and when different project histories are compared. There is universal agreement that data processing ran into trouble after the first euphoria because management did not get sufficiently involved. The defense frequently used pitted the technologists and their jargon against management and their naiveté. Effective management control requires the existence of an application development cycle with an investment in management resources in proportion to the cost of development.

Management of Change

A problem that recurs frequently is how to handle the changes that typically appear during the project development process. Again, it must be stressed that the more complex and expensive the process, the more management control is necessary. Changes in the initial concept are unavoidable and even desirable as developers get deeper into the construction phase. Typical comments heard from groups participating in the development of a needed application are: "If they only stopped changing things, I could get the job done, but you can't expect me to hit a moving target." Or, "They told me they wanted to know what I did and how I did it and now they won't even listen when I explain things better." The management of change requires set points in time for both the developers and users of applications to express themselves. They are both correct. The application development cycle can help define the time and place that each of these two groups can use to be heard.

There has been a great deal said about bringing computational power to individuals and making the development process for some applications extremely short. This process will continue indefinitely and the "fourth-generation" languages, which permit some applications to be developed in a faster, mechanized manner, will become standard tools for the manipulation of information. The large system will remain, and the large application will require the use of application phases and the management control that this approach allows.

The Economics of Application Development

The concept of the application development cycle, introduced in the previous section, will now be expanded upon. One could argue that management control and change procedures, theoretically, depend on a standard definition of the application development process, and if we are to succeed in persuading people to adopt an approach directed at controlling application development, this argument must be made more concrete. Each of the aspects of application development must be placed on a sound economic basis so that a rational choice of whether to implement a system can be made. The resources consumed in the development of useful applications are scarce resources, and economics provides a way of comparing different ways of using these resources and hence of making choices.

The Phases of the Development Life Cycle

Table 7.1 gives the names of some of the steps that we must go through to produce an application. These steps are pictured graphically in Figure 7.3, which exhibits the resources consumed over the lifetime of a development project. In this view the vertical axis represents the number of people working on a project over time. Beginning with only a few people, we slowly increase the number as the details get filled in. In this manner we can determine the advisability of committing resources as we complete our understnnding of what has to be done. On this plot the approximate locations and names of the development phases have been added, with the boundaries drawn at an angle to show that it is possible to have overlapping functions on larger projects. The general shape of this curve, with its slow build-up of resources, is accepted as representing an efficient way to staff a development project if waste is to be avoided.

Systems Planning. The interface with the strategic planning process occurs within the systems planning phase. Plans directed from the top get translated into "actionable" items, and requests surfacing from the operating units either get referred to strategic planning, if they have a large impact, or are decided at their originating level if their effect is small. The exact location within each organization that a "yes" or "no"

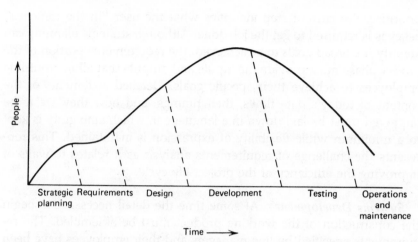

Figure 7.3. The application development process, people vs time.

decision is made about a project is a matter of local standards and procedures. The most important thing to consider, however, is that the knowledge that a particular course of action has been undertaken and will be in place at a future date needs to pass through the systems planning phase so that the effect on future development can be gauged. Some choices, though small in cost, have very widespread effects once they are in place.

The first phase of development must also show that the application seems to be possible technically, will roughly provide the services required, and is probably a worthwhile investment. The terminology used is inexact because at this stage of operation we are dealing with a first estimate which *must* be reexamined at the end of each development phase. The idea that a large project can be conceived of, developed, and delivered by an absentee development team taking one or more years to produce it is simply incorrect. Organizations and their environments change faster than multiyear development projects can be completed. The best approach is incremental, which implies that the output of the feasibility study will be a long-term document that gets revisited periodically.

Systems Requirements. The systems requirements stage is the time at which a first cut of some of the detail required by the end user is specified. The previous step identified organizational objectives and priorities; the current step identifies what the user "in the trenches" believes is required to get the job done. Although strategic planning can identify the broad goals to be achieved, the requirements portion of the project phase must provide the inputs and outputs that allow front-line employees to achieve their specific goals. Detailed statements of the content of today's data flows, their timings, and how they are to be improved must be laid down in a language in which ambiguity is kept to a minimum while flexibility of expression is maintained. This represents the challenge of requirements analysis as it relates to ways of improving the efficiency of the project life cycle.

Systems Development. At some time the detail necessary to begin the construction of the working product must be assembled. The requirements specified by line managers and their employees have been integrated with the requirements specified by the organization as a whole. Now we must marry these to the constraints of the physical environment in which the system will operate to produce the system specifications. It is necessary to include hardware limitations and the complex set of jigsaw puzzle interfaces specified by any software already working. The defacto standards established by code sets previously defined and data that are already part of the existing programs also form the environment that must be taken into account.

Now the data processing professional begins to play a dominant role. The practical requirements of building a program begin to compromise the intellectual structure built according to the grand design. It is in this way that systems diverge from the targets set for them. Management must control most strongly when development begins, for it is here that the data processing specialist can misread and affect the importance of a particular operation.

The methodology that an organization chooses for its development either enhances or retards management's ability to keep track of the system design. Obviously the larger the design the greater the need for a strong development methodology. Yet just as when travelling by car the greatest danger occurs on the small trips where we spend most of our time, so it is that in small applications the need for protection is greatest. Much of the effort devoted to the development of applications produces small programs that are only used a few times. These programs are rarely tested adequately and disappear long before the problems they cause appear. The software development methodology chosen must fit in with the strategic planning approach and the systems analysis methodology we choose. The literature abounds with techniques, each emphasizing some view on how systems ought to be built, and management must understand how each can be integrated with already existing approaches to improve the way we control our electronic data processing resources. The latter half of the system development phase concerns itself with the architectural approach we choose to build our systems.

Systems Implementation. The fourth phase of the development cycle, as depicted in Table 1, concerns itself with integrating the new application into the ongoing daily work of our organizations. Nothing ever stands still. We must run alongside, comparing our new, better model, with the old tested procedures. When we are certain that we can do at least as well as before, we can begin to replace the old with the new with some degree of confidence. There will be problems, and programs and procedures will need to be modified. Again, difficult tradeoffs between what can be done and what ought to be done will be made by the data processing professionals and the line employees. Once more, control is essential or the design integrity and purpose built into the systems design will begin to evaporate. A well-understood and uniformly applied methodology is still the key to controlling the purpose of our systems.

Systems Maintenance. If the system survives to become part of the ongoing operations of our organization by being both useful and acceptable, we enter a new phase of operation. The maintenance of the software and how to approach it is perhaps the most difficult of all the practical problems that face us. Each year as more and more software becomes a crucial part of our environment, the inventory of components that must be maintained grows. In the past, it was common to blame programmers for the increasing budget of the maintenance function, in the belief that it was carelessness or incompetence that led to software errors. However, detailed studies of the elements of the software budget have led to other conclusions. Larry Putnam[4] is an advocate of a class of dynamic models that simulate the life cycle of applications programs. These are statistical averages of the behavior of ideal projects. In his models the *most* we can hope to do is to spend 39% of the total life-cycle costs on development and the remaining 61% on maintenance. The literature contains many examples and reports of other splits of 70/30%, 80/20%, and more. One evaluation of different life-cycle cost methodologies complained that the Putnam model uniformly underestimated the maintenance cost by a factor of from two to four. Numbers like these begin to explain what has been going on in the relative portions of data processing budgets.

The software maintenance process seems to contain three separate components.[5] There are bonafide errors that must be fixed; there are evolutionary changes that occur in our organizations that must be taken into account; and finally there are changes mandated by legislation. Only the first of these appears to come from poor programming, whereas the latter two are environmental changes that all organizations must worry about. It is no wonder that a dynamic evolutionary model predicts a 40/60% split between development and maintenance costs.

Mandated changes occur whenever an organization must satisfy a new regulation. For example, whenever Congress changes the tax and social security structure, each payroll program in the United States must be updated. The process of changing an already existing program is a more error-prone operation than writing a program from scratch. Thus, the maintenance process helps to feed the cost problems of software development. The payroll example is only the tip of the iceberg. The expense, for instance, associated with Universal Product Codes, the necessity of keeping track of each of the automobile owners and the changes in related regulations on a periodic basis make mandated programs a very important component of the software development budget.

The second component we mentioned was the evolutionary changes that an organization goes through over the years. When products change, their new characteristics have to be added to the already existing programs. If the code numbers assigned to a product increase by a single character or digit, all the programs that refer to them must change. If a company reorganizes its geographical distribution so that it has districts as well as regions, many of its programs need to be changed. Each time a program is changed, whatever design integrity it had from its first construction gets diffused, the next change gets harder, and the maintenance part of the budget increases.

The remaining component of the maintenance budget does stem from errors, but, again, the programmer is wrongfully maligned. If we look at which phase in the application development life cycle could possibly be the source of the malfunction we discover that better than 50% of the problems detected stem from ambiguities or misunderstandings that were generated sometime in the requirements stage or strategic planning of the system. This has been true historically for all types of programs.

What we are left with after an examination of the sources of maintenance problems is the realization that each of the three types of maintenance components would be under better control if a strong, well-understood methodology had been in place during the development life cycle. If a program's structure is under control, then the insertion of different functions can be done in a controlled fashion. We can know every place where a potential effect can occur. If a controlled methodology had been in place, then the requirements process could be traced back so that each of the misunderstandings could be examined to see what consequences they had. The conclusions seem inescapable. A disciplined approach, any disciplined approach, is essential. Management must help choose the approach that fits in best with the existing disciplines of strategic planning and requirements analysis.

Thus we have the phases of the development life cycle. If you feel that some other set of names describes, reasonably well, what your organization does, then feel free to choose a set different from the examples shown in Tables 7.1 and 7.2. The crucial idea is that you must choose some set of names and functions, and you must stick with them until it is painfully clear that you gain much more from the new formulation than you lose by dislocating your organization and perhaps invalidating your laboriously accumulated statistics.

Financial Justification

Planning structures and systems life cycles need to contain related steps that verify and validate previous work. Systems planning requires this combination also and has an appropriately related pair of steps. The first is linkage to the strategic and tactical planning of the organization, the second is a feasibility study. A feasibility study attempts to show that the developer and the user of an application both understand the functions to be carried out and have come to a common understanding of what should be done. The user attests to the appropriateness of the application, while the developer attests to the ability to do what has been laid out. This combination gives a measure of confidence that the application can be done and that it will succeed in carrying out a useful service.

The remaining question is whether it is worthwhile to do. This determination is the financial justification of the application. The logic of economic justification is simple; it is the carrying out of the logic in practice that is difficult. In principle, once an independent business function of an organization is defined, we determine what its money flows are today. We combine the cost of carrying out that function with the benefits that the function brings in, regardless of whether it is profit or nonprofit. If there are no flows inward, then we are considering a cost center or service component of the organization. In the early years of data processing, because almost all the applications considered dealt with administrative functions, the usual model did not mention revenue flows inward.

The next step in the process is to make an estimate of the same business component after the procedures have been changed and the system installed and operating on a daily basis. We sum up exactly the same components. In this manner we arrive at functions that can be compared. Often the estimate includes an extrapolation to a future environment where, either because of an increase in business volume, or because the work to be carried out has grown more complex, or both, the current way of operating has become too expensive. When a comparison can be based on the same end products, even when estimates are involved, then rational decisions on what to automate can be made.

The procedures we must put into place to arrive at that future operating environment will cost something. This cost represents our investment in a new operating environment and must be compared with alternative investments that are available to us. Opportunity costs become especially important when we are resource limited in what we would like to accomplish. Some objective measure needs to be applied so that we can choose among possible uses of our scarce data processing resources.

Whatever measure we choose varies, depending on the complexity of the environment and the scope of the application being considered. In the most straightforward circumstance, there are no revenue flows inward and the costs of the business function are well understood. This

Table 7.3. Analysis of Cash Flows in an Investment Decision.

		Year				
	1983	1984	1985	1986	1987	1988
Current proce-dures	240,000	270,000	350,000	370,000	388,000	407,000
Proposed proce-dures	240,000	270,000	283,000	297,000	312,000	327,000
Development costs	(100,000)	(100,000)				
Savings			67,000	73,000	76,000	80,000
Cumulative cash flow	(100,000)	(200,000)	(133,000)	(60,000)	16,000	96,000

is the simplest place to begin to discuss the popular measures that can be used to decide the merits of a particular application.

Consider the example in Table 7.3. A department is operating at a level in which the net cash flows show a cost of $240,000 in the current year, with an estimated growth to over $400,000 in the next five years. An analysis of the department's operations shows that the increasing volumes and complexity of operations will require additional people in two years, which accounts for the sudden spurt in expenses. The manager of the department has proposed the installation of data processing equipment and the writing of a program that will increase the productivity of the current personnel to avoid hiring new employees. The cost of the new equipment and the programs will be $100,000 for each of the two years of development. Should the firm proceed with the investment? The figures in Table 7.3 show the accumulated cash flows, including the investments and the resulting less-expensive operating environment. According to this analysis, the firm begins to show an accumulated positive cash position for this investment in the third year of operation. The pay-back period for the investment is three years. Comparisons can be made based on pay-back period, and if a particular threshold is exceeded, the application ought to be attempted.

This method of selection does not lend itself to comparison with alternative, long-term investments. It is a binary choice with little in the way of shades of gray available.

A second approach attempts to look at the stream of cash flows and compare them at a particular instant in time. Money earned four years from now has a different value than money spent today. The mental model we apply pictures a sum of money deposited in an interest-bearing account that grows to a particular value at some point in the future. This approach, known as *net present value of money*, begins with an assumed rate of interest for each time period (it need not remain the same) and calculates how much money would have to be on deposit at the start of the investment to reach a given figure in a target year. As an example, if the interest rate were 20% and the target value in 2 years were $50,000, then we would have to have $34,722 on deposit today. Using the figures in Table 7.3 we can compute the net present value of the cash stream given, with investments subtracted and increases in cash flows added. The result, using an interest rate of 10% and depicted in Table 7.4, shows a net present value of $19,059. The cash flow estimates should be made to extend to the life of the program with declining net present values for each of the years. A simple criterion is: If the net present value is positive, proceed; if not, do not begin.

The third approach looks on the costs incurred in the creation of a new application as an investment. The savings realized by that application represent the interest earned on that deposit. It is possible to calculate the rate of return on the investment that best approximates the revenue flow described by the savings. Table 7.5 shows this approximation for the example we have been using. The internal rate of return is a measure which can be used to compare alternative investment strategies, including doing nothing but leaving the money in the bank. The internal rate of return is related to the organization's cost of capital and

Table 7.4.   Analysis of Net Present Values in an Investment Decision.

To Have a Savings of	In Year (Years) from Now	Invest Today (Net Present Value)
80,000	1988 (6)	45,157
76,000	1987 (5)	47,190
73,000	1986 (4)	49,900
67,000	1985 (3)	50,338
(100,000)	1984 (2)	(82,644)
(100,000)	1983 (1)	(90,909)
96,000		$19,059

Table 7.5. Analysis of Internal Rate of Return in an Investment Decision.

$$200,000 = \frac{45,157}{(1 + i)^6} + \frac{47,190}{(1 + i)^5} + \frac{49,900}{(1 + i)^4} + \frac{50,338}{(1 + i)^3} + \cdots$$

serves a useful function when considering very large investments. A recent estimate of the value expended by some corporations in creating, keeping, and using database systems is in the billions of dollars.

Risk and Uncertainty. The decision on which course of action to pursue depends on the certainty with which we predict future events, something we usually cannot do well at all. At best we can identify several alternative scenarios that represent views of the future. What should the approach to justification be in these circumstances? This dilemma is analogous to the dilemma faced by gamblers in a gambling casino. That is not to say that economic justification is related to gambling directly, but there are some comparisons that ought to be made. For one, all casinos set up circumstances in which they cannot lose over the long run. The fairest casinos have zero sum games, where each side would break even if they played for an infinitely long period of time. The justification scenario postulates a "game" in which the systems analysts and designers try to stack the odds in their favor. This analysis comes directly out of game theory.

In each circumstance an attempt is made to list the probable scenarios and to estimate the probability of each scenario's occurring. The complete analysis is made for each of the options, and a weighted average of the measures is calculated. Table 7.6 looks at three alternatives for

Table 7.6. Example of a Risk Assessment Based on Cumulative Cash Flow.

Alternative	Risk	1988 Cumulative Cash Flow ($)
1	.80	96,000
2	.15	−20,000
3	.05	200,000

Avg. Cumulative Cash Flow = .8 × (96,000) + .15 × (−20,000) + .05 × (200,000)
= 83,800

the example used previously. The first alternative is the one given in Table 7.3; the second assumes that the cost of producing the application extends into the third year in such a way that there is a net outflow of capital for that year. The final choice assumes that we overestimated the difficulty and that we have achieved some benefit in the second year. The analyst assigns a relative probability to each of these occurrences of 80, 15, and 5%, respectively. The weighted sum of the measures in then shown in Table 7.6.

A comparison between alternative investment strategies produces two competing approaches, depending on one's assessment of where the risk really lies. In some instances a set of ground rules is made, wherein a probability of failure greater than some number, 20%, say, is automatic grounds for not doing a project.

Tangible and Intangible Cash Flows.   The previous analysis assumes the simplest of all possible circumstances. Each of the costs and benefits associated with an application is assumed to be quantifiable, which is usually not the case. Early investment in management information systems was conveniently justified with the phrase, "improved management decision making." This phrase quieted the uneasy feelings caused by the lack of understanding of exactly what was to be accomplished and, perhaps even more important, the absence of any real information about the way decision making occurs. As an example, some people believe that the introduction of professional-based office systems, which include a terminal on each professional's desk, does not improve the speed at which documents are produced. The professional begins to become concerned with form as well as content, and the time saved is consumed by issues which did not previously exist.

The effect of intangible cash flows into and out of a department or function can either be caused by increasing revenue or by decreasing costs. The previous example described an intangible *benefit* that was questioned. There can also be intangible *costs* that must be questioned. As an example, consider a patient billing system in a hospital whose designers assumed that there are only a small number of generic insurance plans. The operational environment that was assumed would exist after system installation provided for a single clerk who would handle the exceptional conditions not covered by the programming.

Upon completion of the system and retirement of that clerk, who had been employed for a considerable period of time, it was discovered that there were many more exceptions than imagined. The retired clerk had been handling them all in an effective manner but the wisdom and lore learned through years of experience were now gone, and now two full-time clerks, rather than one, were required. In this example the costs of running the department were underestimated because something intangible, experience, was neglected.

The certainty of justification analysis disappears as the number of intangible estimates increase. The accuracy of the measure of comparison decreases until statistically there is no discernable difference, for instance, between an application with an internal rate of return of 12% and one with an internal rate of return of 10%.

System Boundaries. The justification techniques described all assume that a neat boundary can be drawn around the system to be created. The cost–benefit study can isolate all the appropriate flows, and effects outside the system can be ignored. This is becoming less true as systems designers approach new horizons of integrated applications, which cross many organizational boundaries. It is becoming impossible to isolate effects to one small area. An electronic mail system is installed throughout a nationally located, multidivisional company. The flows of information cross every organizational boundary and affect the operations of diverse components. Is there any way of calculating the total cost–benefit status of that application? It can only be estimated, and the true numbers will be revealed by the bottom line of the company's financial report. But then we must isolate this application from all the other causes that combine to create the company's final report—an extremely difficult task.

A recent compendium of papers on the economics of information processing contained a section on the economic factors used in justifying information systems. Two papers in particular considered the problems associated with applications whose exact scope could not be identified. The first, by Scheer,[6] suggested that one way to determine the effects of a particular change was to simulate the business function under discussion. If the simulation seems to describe the current circumstance in a reasonable fashion, then introduce the proposed change and determine the performance of that same business function according to the simulation. In this way we "measure" the economic effects of the change.

A second paper by Bender,[7] suggested that we could identify some large-scale system variables that would characterize systems whose performance was dramatically improved by the introduction of an automated decision system. Bender studied 74 applications and classified them by:

1. *System complexity* based on the number of variables that need to be taken into account in the decision.

2. Management quality based on the scope and quality of things such as planning, forecasting, technical innovation, and the speed of adaptation to new conditions.

In evaluating these applications Bender rated the two attributes as either *hi* or *lo*. The financial improvement factor of each application was known, and when the averages were computed in each of the four possible combinations of *system complexity* and *management quality*, clear differences were evident. The plot is reproduced in Figure 7.4.

The applications which fall into the upper left quadrant, where system complexity is hi and management quality is lo, all showed the highest average profit improvement, whereas those in the other quadrants showed smaller profit improvements. The justification approach implied by this technique characterizes a business application by two variables, complexity and management quality; charts which quadrant this places the application in; and, if the average profit improvement factor implies a good investment, suggests that the application ought to be attempted.

Notice how far we have come from the rational analysis of cost justification. The closer we get to broad applications, crossing organizational boundaries, and affecting complex areas, the less we are able to use simple approaches. Applications that assume white-collar productivity improvement as justification for their implementation are particularly susceptible to difficulties in justification. At the center of this issue is a means for defining productivity increases in business professionals or office workers since there is little in the way of agreed-on measures of performance. It is these measures that are always used to verify the increases in output and from that the cost effectiveness of the change

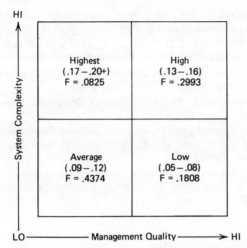

Figure 7.4. Magnitude of profit improvement.

in procedure. There are many problems with understanding how to improve the efficiency of this type of work, not the least of which is the lack of repeatability of the tasks. The before and after comparisons that have always enabled us to decide between alternatives disappear. Because no two circumstances are identical, comparisons are never totally clear.

In the areas where we cannot use a simple calculation, we inevitably make an entrepreneurial decision on the level of risk we are prepared to assume. The circle has been closed. This should not imply that justification is futile and need not be done. The decision must be made on the basis of as much information as is possible. But in application justification as in much of decision making, there is no replacement for the informed judgment of knowledgeable practitioners in the field. The numbers gathered during the justification exercise help us to understand the function we are studying and protect us from silly errors of judgment.

REFERENCES

1. Naumann, J. D., and Jenkins, A. M., "Prototyping: The New Paradigm for Systems Development," *Management Information Systems Quarterly*, vol. 6, no. 3, 1982.

2. Biggs, C. L., Birks, E. G., and Atkins, W. A., *Managing the Systems Development Process*, Prentice-Hall, Englewood Cliffs, NJ, 1980.

3. Cotterman, W. W., Couger, J. D., Enger, N. L., and Harold, F. (eds.), *Systems Analysis and Design: A Foundation for the 1980s*, Elsevier, North-Holland, 1981.

4. Putnam, L. H., *Tutorial Software Cost Estimating and Life-Cycle Control: Getting the Software Numbers*, IEEE Computer Society, New York, 1980.

5. Lientz, B., and Swanson, E., *Software Maintenance Management*, Addison-Wesley, Reading, MA, 1980.

6. Scheer, A. W., "Assessing the Economy of Computer-Based Information Systems," in R. Goldberg and H. Lorin (eds.), *The Economics of Information Processing*, vol. 1, Wiley, New York, 1982.

7. Bender, P. S., "Measuring the Value of Automated Decision Support Systems," in R. Goldberg and H. Lorin (eds), *The Economics of Information Processing*, vol. 1, Wiley, New York, 1982.

QUESTIONS FOR THOUGHT

1. Tables 7.1 and 7.2 show two possible sets of names for application development phases. Can you come up with other sets of names which break application development steps differently?

2. Assume that you are part of a manufacturing organization. One of the jobs is to make certain that there is always enough raw material available, acquired at the best possible price, to fill production needs. To that end one member of the staff buys and sells raw material contracts on the commodity exchanges. The professional in this position has been doing that job successfully and within the last year a decision support system was installed to support the work. Recently, this decision maker has requested a substantial investment in new equipment to upgrade the available data processing facilities supporting that function. The executive supporting that function has asked you to come up with a cost justification for the request. What should you do and how do you determine whether the investment is justified?

8

Detailed Systems Analysis: Methodologies

The apparent importance of having a methodology to direct tasks related to computers dates from the beginning of automated data processing. The large number of disastrous war stories that came from the early years of application development led people to believe that there existed a magical approach, which when applied according to the rules, would guarantee success. When the method used today failed to provide the magic, designers and managers looked for some other, newer, better approach.

After the feasibility analysis is complete, it is time to assemble the approaches that will lead to a working program. It is at this point in the application development cycle that the chosen methodology begins to dictate the next set of steps to be followed, and it is here that the project manager must decide which of the touted methodologies should be used. Some organizations choose a method for everyone and all projects; others allow local discretion, giving each systems analyst and programmer or manager free rein in deciding which approach to use.

THE ROLE OF A METHODOLOGY

A methodology is a fixed set of procedures that directs a group of users through the set of steps that they will perform. A methodology tells its users what to do next. In the discussion on information systems planning, a distinction was made between strong and weak approaches. Here too when dealing with design methodologies, a similar distinction is relevant. The relationship between strong and weak methodologies implied a tendency to either be concerned with problem formulation and identification of the "disease" that has caused the current problem, or to be concerned with arriving at a solution to the problems currently at hand. When choosing which systems analysis and design approach one ought to follow, a similar tendency exists. The problem-oriented approaches are procedurally oriented, and the solution-oriented approaches seem to be driven by currently used data structures. Just as in information systems planning one could choose from a spectrum of techniques, so too in systems analysis and design methodologies one can choose from among a spectrum of techniques.

Process decomposition, which refers to those approaches that analyze and understand what is done, attempts to explain the steps in minute detail. A technique that uses this approach is stepwise refinement. The approaches that use the natural flow of data through a problem to determine the structure of the design are called structured techniques; representative of this class are the approaches of Yourdon[1] and Myers.[2] The third approach looks at the structure of a set of data items required in the solution and provides a system or program with a similar form that can create the solution. These are the techniques of Jackson,[3,4] Warnier,[5] and Warnier-Orr.[6]

An added dimension that design approaches provide in this spectrum of techniques is the formality of the language used to describe the design. We have stressed the detail that systems analysis must provide if a system is to be written. When an examination is made of the causes of failure in past projects, clearly inadequate design is a major villain. Whatever design methodology is chosen must include strategies for keeping track of the detail contained in a completed design, and that implies a way of expressing and communicating the design to others. Just as a spectrum of techniques exists, there also exists a spectrum of notational approaches which vary in intent and applicability.

The natural language which people use to talk to each other is a highly ambiguous and *informal* mechanism for transmitting design information. It has the advantage that most programmers and analysts can use it well enough to be understood, but it pays a price by being imprecise. When a designer writes a series of words to describe a design, we can consider it to be in an informal language.

Natural language is possessed of at least two general properties: It has a grammar, and it has semantics. Grammar refers to the rules of connection between kinds of words and ideas, and semantics refers to the ideas contained within those words. We can construct sentences in a language that obey all the grammatical rules, but connect words unrelated to each other and therefore have no meaning. It is easier to check a sentence for grammatical rules than for an understandable meaning. One way to create a language in which the ambiguity is limited is to define its grammar. In this, limiting the rules connecting the elements of the design eliminates a degree of ambiguity. A natural language, such as English, does have a grammar also, but because of its flexibility and varied use, is not limited at all. The *formatted* language constructed by identifying grammatical rules of construction is much less ambiguous and therefore (it is assumed) leads to better, cleaner designs.

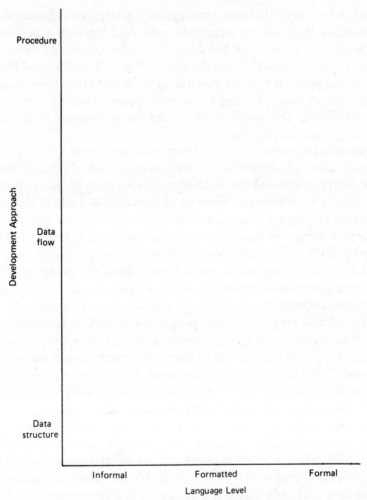

Figure 8.1.   Possible design approaches.

Finally, if some means of expressing the semantics of the design in a language is available, we can further limit the ambiguity present and provide even better designs. These languages are called *formal* languages. The formal languages require training in both a semantic component and a grammatical component, whereas the formatted languages require only grammatical training and the informal languages no training at all. A tradeoff is established between the level of training and the ambiguity present in the description. It seems to follow from this that the informal languages are the most easily read, whereas the formal languages are the ones least read.

The two variables of language and design approach sketch out a table, which is shown in Figure 8.1.

As an example of how to place a techniques on this chart let us place those discussed in information systems planning. SADT is driven by a

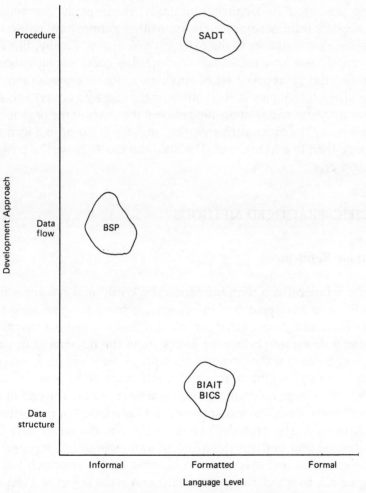

Figure 8.2. Relationship between information systems planning approaches.

hierarchic decomposition of the procedure. This would place it vertically near the top of the chart. Its language is constrained by the grammar of the box and arrow language, but it is not analyzed semantically to see if there is in fact a relationship between the identified figures. It is a formatted language.

BSP, business systems planning, looks at the information flows of an organization as expressed by the process–database relationship. The flows linking these processes are the transaction triggers of the information systems that support the general manager. This places BSP among the data flow languages vertically. Horizontally, the language type appears informal since there are neither grammatical constraints, nor semantic constraints to the resulting description. Finally, BIAT and BICS are driven by a particular structure, the order configuration, to determine the appropriate set of applications for an organization. This places these techniques at the bottom of the chart vertically, and since there is a constrained relationship between the states of the organization as defined by the order attributes, the language is closer to a formatted language than to a formal one. The filled-out chart shows the positions (Figure 8.2).

SPECIFIC, PRACTICED METHODS

Stepwise Refinement

Stepwise refinement is a term introduced by Wirth[7] and has come to include the general approach of top-down structured programming.[8] The phrase *refinement*, as used in this context, refers to a process that grinds something down into ever finer pieces, as in the refinement of sugar. The procedures that the designer attempts to carry out on a computer are analyzed by starting from a global statement of purpose or intent, which is then broken down into finer and finer pieces. The end of each step leaves the designer with a more exact description of the system to be constructed. The procedure ends when all of the terms have been fully defined and perhaps described in a programming language that can be compiled and executed. An example of this approach is given in Figure 8.3, in which the game of checkers is the object of a stepwise refinement process. The highest level of the procedural decomposition

```
Checkers:
    Choose_sides
    Setup_the_Board
    Make_moves until (no_longer_possible)
    Either Congratulate-the_Winner
    Or Call_it_a_Draw
End Checkers
```

Figure 8.3. Stepwise refinement of the game of checkers. First refinement.

begins with nothing more than the rulebook for checkers and an awareness of the sequence of play. The analyst begins by identifying the set of steps we go through to play checkers. First sides are chosen, with one name assigned to each of the opposing sides. The second step in the process is to set up the data structures that will represent the board. Most of the action occurs in the sequence of alternating moves, which terminates with one of the two opponents being unable to make a legal move. This situation occurs when there are no pieces left, with the result that a winner is determined, or there are no more legal moves to be made with some pieces available, in which as there is a draw. Notice that the sequence of steps defined so far hardly even made reference to the rulebook and defers all specific decisions to a later time. Still, the flow of the procedure is accurately depicted.

The second stage in the process is to breakup the terms already identified into their constituent parts. In this second stage of the decomposition, more detail will be required (Figure 8.4). In the second refinement, some more of the logic required by the game has been revealed. The notion of "no pieces remaining for either black or red" is required to help decide whether the Make_moves logic terminates. During the second refinement, no real program logic is introduced. Those who have some experience in the writing of programs will notice that the structure can be formalized considerably and in the process economies of definition can be introduced, for example, by generalizing the idea of a move so that a single set of terms describes either the red move or the black move. As systems design proceeds, some backtracking is inevitable to continue the design; but if done carefully and maintained, then a record of the thought process entering the design becomes a part of the design library.

The idea of stepwise refinement is also referred to by the phrase *top-*

```
Make_moves
    if possible than accept_move_from_red
    Check_the_board
    If legal_move proceed
    otherwise try_again
    if black_pieces_all_gone
        then no_longer_possible
    if possible then accept_move_from_black
    Check_the_board
    If legal_move proceed
    otherwise try_again
    if red_pieces_all_gone
        then no_longer_possible
    make_another_pair_of_moves
End Make_moves
```

Figure 8.4. Stepwise refinement of the game of checkers. Second refinement.

down design (or programming). This name implies that systems are designed from the top-most cause or reason, with the sequence of steps proceeding in a manner that keeps that initial reason as its source and simply clarifies the corresponding ideas to the point of complete understanding. Those parts still described in a language that does not lead to potential machine execution are replaced one at a time. The casual reader can pick up the description at any point and work down, continuously, to whatever level of detail seems to be appropriate.

Stepwise refinement is most closely related to the SADT analysis technique, which we discussed among the information systems planning techniques. It is driven by the decomposition of the procedure of the problem, which is expressed in a language that usually begins as a very close derivative of natural English. These characteristics help to place it in the upper left-hand corner of the methodology chart (Figure 8.1).

Stepwise refinement is the most general of the problem-solving methodologies. The approach it recommends has been used as a way of analyzing problems in all areas of human endeavor, and its reformulation to refer specifically to the computer environment should come as no surprise. It is therefore consistent with many corporate strategic planning disciplines and should be understandable to representatives of both the corporate planning community and the information systems planning community.

Composite/Structured Design and Analysis

The ideas of composite and structured analysis are among the most popular of the analysis and design methodologies. In the view of this approach, the fundamental concept is that a system ought to be driven by how data flows through the problem area. If the designer is able to model this flow, then the decomposition introduced will be a natural one, and any necessary evolutionary changes will fit very nicely into the original decomposition. The divide-and-conquer strategy is still the driving force, but the points of division are identified along the data stream of the problem area.

The parallel idea in strategic planning is to concentrate on the analysis of organizational structure, which sometimes accompanies strategic planning. Just as the structure of an organization should reflect the information flows that are required to support its business, so too, the information flows required in a system should support the systems structure required to provide a particular function. Just as the organizational components break along information flow boundaries, so too, a system's components should break where information flows change their nature. The parallel continues when information standards that an auditing function establishes are considered. In much the same way that the definition of items and time durations must be established across an organization's components to avoid confusion, the data items used by a system must also be well understood and guarded, to avoid confusion and difficulties within a computerized system.

The key design ideas that emerge from this parallel view are those of modularity, guidelines for identifying the shape of the components into which the system is partitioned, and the analysis approach. Modularity is an attribute of the static state of the system, and the analysis approach shapes the dynamic flow of the system. The combination of these two aspects helps to fully define the kind of system we end up producing, but they must be understood independently.

Modularity. Few computer theoreticians today believe in creating systems which do not have many independent pieces that fit together to make the whole. This is one of the first ideas to emerge from the early days of computer science. What was absent in those early days was a set of principles that could be used to guide what should go into a module. The composite/structured design (CSD) advocates recognized that a module could be described using two independent attributes. The first dealt with how unique and single-minded a purpose the module was called on to serve—its "strength." The second dealt with its communication to the world outside its boundaries—its "cohesion" (or coupling).

The concept of strength arose from the observation that whenever a module was called on to perform disparate functions, there was an increased chance that a casual mix-up would have far-removed consequences. If the range of functions could be narrowed, the scope of the module's effect could also be narrowed. As a consequence, a problem that arises can easily be isolated to the general area in which it occurs. The approach identified various gradations of "goodness" on the basis of how narrowly the function accomplished by the module is defined. An equivalent way to describe these gradations is in terms of the words used to describe the module's function, that is, the transformation that the module is called upon to effect. If the designer can describe this function in a simple English language sentence, with no use of connectives such as *and, if, then* or *but*, then a module with functional strength has been used, which is good. However, if some of these connectives were necessary, then a less than optimal set has been used and the designer ought to understand why a departure from functional strength was the best approach.

Information Hiding.   The other attribute of modules, cohesion, refers to the manner in which a system communicates its internal data. This is the data required as intermediate steps in the production of the files and reports that are a system's outputs. Just as it is poor practice to allow unrestricted access to all files and reports without some need to know, so, too, is it poor systems design practice to allow every component of a system to have access to all of the intermediate data items used in that system. Systems have tables, pointers, constants, and intermediate calculations, to name only a few, that are used over and over in the operations of a single system invocation. If the names are universally known, then any module can accidentally, or on purpose, pick out a piece of program data and use it. This has the advantage that it becomes easier for programmers to get at control information they need to do certain of their bookkeeping operations, and is a more time efficient way to send data around.

The disadvantages of this approach are that inadvertent mix-ups change highly unexpected areas of a program. The global use of data makes the understanding of the design very difficult because hidden effects in other places change values when we are not looking. By way of analogy, this circumstance would be something like living in a house and attempting to read in one room while the lights went off and on randomly because the electrician had decided to cross all the power lines to make the job of wiring easier. By not having to leave the central wiring room, he would save many steps in getting the house wired.

The CSD approach recommends that global data should never be used. Each module should only have the right to use those items directly required for its operation. Although the idea of strength was accepted as reasonable almost immediately, the concept of only allowing local data to be defined in a complex system has been met with much skepticism. System designers have believed that such an arrangement would so impair the efficiency of operation that almost all execution would be impossible. Besides, they said, all the older systems have been built with so much global information that it is impossible to refit them without an extremely large investment in new software design. Thus, although the ideas of CSD have been with us for a great many years, it is only now and only to a limited degree that cohesion is being accepted in practice.

Structured Systems Analysis.   Structured systems analysis is a data-directed, engineering-oriented approach to systems analysis that was developed in the mid-to-late 1970s. There are several texts on the subject by DeMarco,[9] Gane and Sarson,[10] and Weinberg,[11] all of which employ the same basic set of concepts and terminology.

Since the term *structured* has become one of the most overutilized words in data processing, one is immediately drawn to wonder about its use here. In fact, this approach, as will be shown, is "structured" in the senses that it is top-down in nature, is designed to be integrated with structured program design techniques, and is a unified approach to solving the systems analysis problem.

Structured systems analysis is, in reality, the marriage of several techniques, some fairly new and some relatively old. The central vehicle is the "data flow diagram" (DFD), which is intended to graphically show the movement of data through a system. Other tools used include "data structure diagrams," decision trees, decision tables, structured English, tight English, data normalization, and data dictionaries.

A DFD is a two-dimensional structure composed of four basic elements: process boxes (represented by vertically oriented, rounded-edge rectangles in the Gane and Sarson style), data stores (open-ended, horizontally oriented rectangles), external entities (squares), and data flow arrows. Process boxes transform data, data stores hold data, data flow arrows facilitate the movement of data, and external entities are the data interfaces with people or systems outside of the present system. Figure 8.5 is an example of a DFD for a car rental company's reservation and billing system.

DFDs are intended to be nonphysical, showing only the flow of information among processes, stores, and external entities, and not showing disks, tapes, CPUs, or any other potential physical implementation vehicles. They are designed to be understandable not only to programmers, but to users as well, in order to facilitate the user feedback process. To that end, one feature of the DFD concept is that the diagrams be drawn in a top-down fashion. The diagram in Figure 8.5 is, admittedly, a high-level view of the system. But it does fulfill two needs. For one thing, it outlines the entire system, and for another, it provides an easy-to-understand entry vehicle for a nonanalytically oriented user.

The diagram in Figure 8.6 is an "explosion" of the Process Reservation process box in Figure 8.5. The process boxes in Figure 8.6, when taken

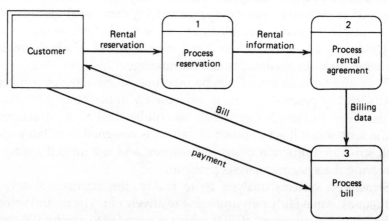

Figure 8.5. Structured systems analysis: Data flow diagram for the car rental reservation system.

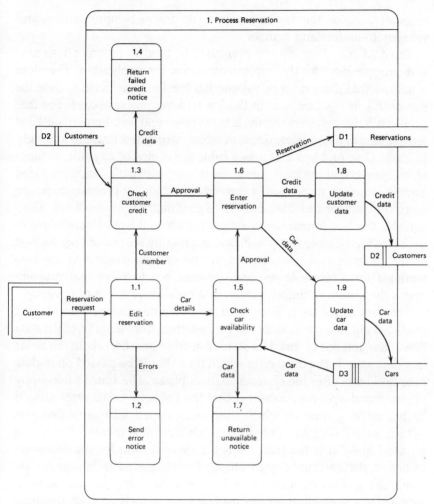

Figure 8.6. Structured systems analysis: Detail of the "Process Reservation" box.

together, describe in further detail the function outlined in the process box in Figure 8.5. The intention is that the process boxes be repeatedly exploded down, creating a hierarchy of process box levels, until each lowest-level process box represents an amount of function equivalent to approximately a module of code (about 50 to 100 lines in a higher-level language) in a structured design sense. Thus, all of the DFDs taken together describe the application in a top-down, comprehensive, and yet easy-to-understand manner.

The data flow diagrams will eventually be used by program designers and programmers for the implementation of the application. Therefore it follows that there must be yet another level of logic detail to describe the details of the functions in the lowest-level process boxes. For that need, structured systems analysis turns to several well-known, detailed techniques: decision trees, decision tables, structured English, and tight English. One problem that arises from the choice of any one of these techniques is that the more formal tools—decision tables and structured English—though more readily converted to code by programmers, are more difficult for uninitiated users to comment on for feedback. Conversely, the less formal tools—decision trees and tight English—make user feedback a more real possibility, but require more work on the part of the programmers. An attempt by the systems analyst to use two methods for a single lowest-level process box to solve that problem opens the question, unfortunately, of a possible problem of integrity.

The data stores are collections of fields of information. Exactly what fields belong in a given store can be discerned from a study of the data flows into and out of that data store. A further question about the fields in a data store is the manner in which they should be passed on to data base designers after the systems analysis phase. The stated philosophy of structured systems analysis is that the fields in a data store should be passed in a form in which they are grouped into simplified sets (which would contain nonredundant data if implemented directly as physical files). It is felt that this is the clearest form for the designers to use in the eventual design phase. The suggested technique for accomplishing this arrangement of fields in a data store is data normalization. Data normalization has usually been associated with database design rather than with systems analysis (and will be discussed in more detail in Chapter 10). But the argument in structured systems analysis is that it should be done here for two reasons. For one thing, data normalization requires a thorough understanding of the true semantic meaning of the fields and the relationships of the fields to each other in this application, an understanding that the systems analyst has at the earliest and at the deepest level. In addition, one of the standard techniques for database design requires data normalization as its first step, regardless of the eventual physical structure used. Thus, if it has to be performed unconditionally, it might as well be done at this stage, even if the eventual physical vehicle has not yet been selected.

The requirement that all of the data flow diagrams and associated information be recorded and maintained suggests a recording method—the data dictionary. This method dictates that the systems analysts be the originator of the items in the dictionary. The items would include the process boxes, data flows, data stores, and external entities, as well as field descriptions. The latter would presumably be used and enhanced by the physical design people at a later time.

As an aid in recording the data access requirements of the application and as an aid in eventual database design, a "data immediate access diagram" or "data structure diagram" can be drawn. It is really an exercise in noting the relationships among entities: Given the value of some item, the appropriate question is, What are the related values of another item.

Another aspect of structured systems analysis is its potential interface with structured system design techniques. As stated earlier, each lowest-level process box is intended to become a module of code in a structured design sense. Thus the program designer is expected to convert the data flow diagram's lowest-level process boxes (and overall logic) into a top-down, modular design. Clearly, the program designer's job is not eliminated. Not only does the program designer have to do the stated conversion, but in addition, the function in some process boxes may have to be combined into a single program module, or, alternately, the function in a single process box may have do be divided among several program modules, all to accommodate the realities of the physical system.

Several items can be noted in terms of the usage of the structured systems analysis techniques relative to standard systems development phases. The most significant of these is that the systems analysts should first develop a DFD of the existing system (if one does not already exist from the time when that system was created), and then later, as the analysis phase progresses and further management approvals are obtained, should develop a DFD of the proposed system. Another point is that a DFD can be subdivided to indicate that a particular physical implementation may only encompass part of the studied application, for economic or other reasons. A third point is that further information can be put into the DFDs in the process boxes in the form of notes that indicate where or how the function was eventually implemented—even after the analysis phase is over.

Relationship to Other Techniques. The structured techniques are most closely related to the approach of Business Systems Planning (BSP). Both techniques look at the flows of information within an organization as a structural indicator of the way in which systems ought to be defined. The structured approaches place themselves among the data flow methodologies on the comparison chart at a vertical position very close to BSP. The language structures used to describe the design contain some graphical organizing ideas and are thus somewhat formatted, a bit more so than the planning approaches. However, the relative freedom in analysis leads to equivalent freedom in the way the software is put together. There is no formal checking of the appropriateness of the functions as they relate to each other, which places CSD in the formatted column, closer to the informal techniques.

Data Structure Driven Programming

The third of the design ideas recognizes that a designer usually begins with a fully specified result. The direction given simply states, "Come up with a final output that contains this information." The tasks then become simply those of tracing the sources of the information required in the given final form and providing an effective manner for combining these sources. The most effective way to put together the required system to produce what is requested is to model the structure of the system on the given structure of the data that the system will produce.

This philosophy led Michael Jackson and Jean-Dominique Warnier to devise the architecture of data-directed design methodologies. An additional impetus was the belief that it is extremely important to come up with a predictable methodology. Jackson patterned his approach so that it would have four attributes:

1. Rationality.
2. Practicality.
3. Doability.
4. Teachability.

A design methodology, to be universally applicable, must have a set of rules that follow one from the other. These rules have to work in real situations, with no exceptions, and they must be teachable. They would have to apply even in some instances where the manner of implementation appeared stilted, which was preferrable to preserving machine efficiency at the cost of universality.

The result of producing a design philosophy based on the current state of the data was an approach very different from the previous techniques described.

Warnier Design Methodology

The Warnier design methodology is a data-driven approach that takes as its theoretical foundation the ideas of sets and their included subsets. Each of the descriptors of a real problem, its output, its input, and even its organizational setting can be placed into a hierarchical organization. The relationship between all of the pertinent hierarchical representations described by the designer becomes the program or system. The inclusion concept supplies the designer with a mold into which the design can be placed. In this way very little gets left out.

The Role of Data. The most important report is chosen as the beginning point and its structure analyzed into a hierarchical structure. The entire report includes every word or number on the sheet, each of which is placed into sequence by noting that the report consists of part a, followed by part b, followed by part c . . . until the end is reached.

An example of this process is shown in the analysis of how a bank might study its checking account reporting system. This begins by first displaying the statement in Figure 8.7 and then breaking the data identified in the report into a logical hierarchical structure. The form that Warnier chose was brackets expanding outward, with more detail being added as the diagram moved away from the name of the data structure being described. A clear distinction is made between the logical data structure and the physical data structure. The logical form includes much of the implicit information of placement that the reader brings to an understanding of the data structure. The logical form includes the alternate information that might be present under particular circum-

Checking Account Statement

S. P. Triplex   June 26, 1985
1939 Brooklyn Place   Account 9987545
Houston, Texas

Opening Balance	Debits	Credits	Closing Balance
3,219.87	1,946.19	1,012.77	2,286.45

* ** *

* ** *

DATE	ITEM	TYPE	BALANCE
5/25	12.50		3,207.37
5/27	110.00		3,097.30
5/27	50.00	ATM DEPOSIT	3,147.30
•	•	•	•
•	•	•	•
•	•	•	•
6/26	77.20		2,286.45

Figure 8.7. Typical monthly checking account statement.

stances, such as errors or malfunctions. In the example in Figure 8.8 of the monthly checking statement, the explosion groups information in their order of precedence. First happenings are listed at the top and final occurrences at the bottom. In this sense, then, the first decomposition of the data structure has a "beginning of statement information," the body of the statement, and the "end of statement information." These items must occur in this order. Each is now decomposed into its constituent pieces by itself. The body of the statement consists of some number of detailed items, with the notation (1,d) indicating that there will be from 1 to d of these detailed items.

The detail is broken down into each set, consisting of a date, between 1 and t transactions on that date, and the balance at the close of business on that date. Finally each transaction is of a particular type, revealed by the decomposition—a check or a deposit or a correction of some type. The notation (0,1) shows that the transaction may or may not be of this type, but it must be among the types listed.

This approach assures the inclusion of all the possibilities indicated on the checking statement. If some particular error condition can possibly occur, the designer is instructed to include it by a (0,1) notation.

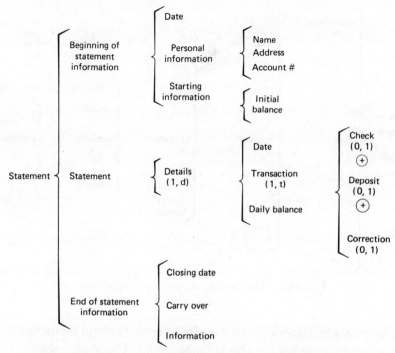

Figure 8.8. Hierarchical decomposition of a checking account statement.

Just as a single report can be analyzed in this fashion, so too the program that produces all reports can be analyzed in this same fashion. The hierarchical breakdown defines the program for each account, included within each branch, included within each monthly period, included within each year. In this way a system for describing a checking account reporting system is defined. The logical position of this subsystem can then be added to all the other subsystems in the bank to create the overall banking system (Figure 8.9).

The Role of time. Time takes on a different meaning in this type of analysis. The diagrams always explicitly include the beginning and ending operations at their top and bottom. The analyst is directed to look at each elementary operation and consider what real-world events could occur at that time that could break the program flow. These are then included as potential logical effects on the data structure used until now.

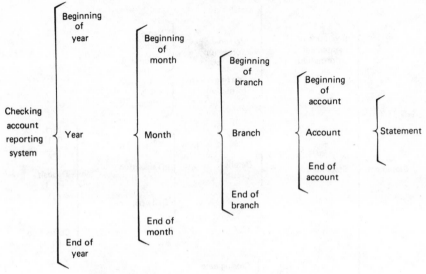

Figure 8.9. The checking account reporting system.

As an example, consider how overdraft checking could be included in the system driven off the checking statement. The logical structure of the daily balance field is modified in Figure 8.10 to seem to include two items, a positive daily balance and a negative daily balance. The positive amount need not be expanded, but the negative one can be rewritten to include either the generation of a loan transaction or a bank error notice. The logic that chooses between the two alternatives, buried in the implicit structure of the logical data structure generated, is coded in as the choice mechanisms that tell what type of transaction is to be done next.

Assembly Line Process.   Systems structure is rounded out by creating the supporting elements to produce the crucial output data structure. The image used is an assembly line where information components are packaged and made ready for the final output operation. In the checking account reporting system, the process begins with the unedited raw transactions: checks, deposits, service charges, automatic transactions, and others of this type. These must be batched together and edited. The assembly line diagram begins with the transactions and then shows the operations required to prepare the transactions for processing. In this

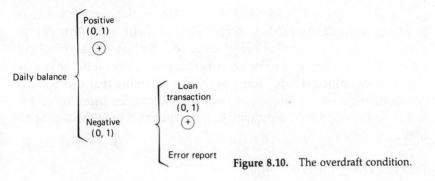

Figure 8.10. The overdraft condition.

case, for example, the transactions might have to be edited for mistakes that are obvious, such as a month code that exceeds 12. This error detection would be a set of programs that always ran before execution of the file updating program, producing edited transactions that might then be sorted. The sorted transactions are part of the input to the statement system, which also requires account information. Accounts are created and eliminated each day, and before today's group is included, there must be a similar assembly line behind it verifying and preparing the information that is included in the account information. In this way the net of supporting operations and flows of information are spread out to design a system that supports the *primary output* of the organization.

The extension of these ideas into the construction of programs uses decision tables, formal Boolean analysis of possible program conditions, and a program design language to express lower-level constructs. Warnier goes through much of this material in his book, which is recommended for readers who are interested in using this method down at the programming level.

Structured Systems Development. The work of Warnier has been extended by Orr into the area that involves database systems in much the same way that the original work of Constantine, Yourdon, and Myers was extended to include data dictionaries and repositories of information. This extension brings the approach a much stronger system flavor and narrows the differences between the proponents of this approach and those convinced that structured analysis is the methodology of choice.

The placement of Warnier and Warnier-Orr on the comparison chart is straightforward. As a data structure method theirs is near the bottom vertically. The absence of a formal language eliminates the formal column and the existence of some grammatical rules places it in the center, closer to the informal side. Some of the formulations that use Boolean notation, higher-level languages, and decision tables bring more formality to the approach, but they are not required if only the essence is used.

Jackson Design Methodology

Jackson design methodology (JDM) starts from the assumption that any programmer should be able to implement the vast majority of data processing tasks in a predictable amount of time. Furthermore the structure of a given program written by two programmers should be essentially the same. A set of steps exists that can be applied in every circumstance that is guaranteed to produce the result requested of the programmer. The approach proceeds by noting that almost every instance in which an analyst or programmer is called upon begins with a statement of what the result is to look like. Invariably it is a particular report that is required. Jackson assumes that once the data structure of this report has been identified, the program to produce it must have a parallel structure. Data exists in three logical forms: sequence, iteration, and selection. In sequence, two items follow each other. In iteration, a particular item is repeated some number of times, and, finally, in selection, a choice is made based on some known criterion. Jackson exhibits a program structure for each of these three ways of organizing a report or data structure. The form of the program is then produced by replacing the structure of the final report with named program items.

The job of the analyst is to develop the output required and structure the set of steps necessary to have all the information on hand at each stage. The programmer uses these structures to do the mechanical translation from the data structure language to the program structure language.

The data structure is treated as a combination of the actual items and how they are stored on physical devices, the alternative possibilities that could exist, and information about the time that information arrives. Errors, for example, are taken into account through the data that are of the selection type. A particular item is identified as being either correct or incorrect, and the program structure then naturally takes the shape of this alternative. The time sequence is also an integral part of the logical data structure where the structure diagram drawn is sequenced in the same order as data is expected to arrive.

Sequential Files. Database management systems stress the ways that data items are related to each other. Each of the vendors has its own proprietary package that structures data as hierarchical forms, network structures, or relational tables. JDM stresses the inherently sequential nature of the way logical data are used. The typical example in Jackson's book is drawn from the world of tape files, which has led some to assume that any other file structure is inaccessible to a Jackson analysis. The intent was to deal with the logical arrival pattern of the data, not its physical file structure. The order in which data arrive is always sequential. The analysts and designers create the physical structure that allows the programmers to access data in any order required, but the systems analyst and users need only think sequentially. This simplifies the mental model of the real process that must be produced to create the program that simulates that process.

The Goals. Jackson believes that the separation of the analysis step from the programming step is a crucial one. The analyst needs to walk in two worlds, the organization's practices and the world of data processing. If there is an imbalance in the training process, then one or the other side has too much emphasis in the system design and an optimal design will not be achieved. The approach of modern software design practices stands on three legs: reliable programs, productivity increases by the development staff, and management's renewed interest in being able to manage the software development business effectively. Jackson emphasizes the last of these as a necessary prerequisite for reliable programs. It is only after management control and reliability has been achieved ought we to concern ourselves with productivity, which will drop automatically from the process.

JDM is the technique that is most data structure driven, and as such is closest to the bottom of the comparison table. The static structure of the final outputs is the chief determinant of the design of the system. Jackson has his own graphical language, which shows the relationship between the three possible data structures and their connections, and he has created a language structure to put into words some of the ways of dealing with the logical alternatives that the data structure can take on. These do not constrain the design process very much, and so, like Warnier and Warnier-Orr's, Jackson's is an example of an almost formatted language.

Some more recent work by Jackson[4] has taken JDM closer to the design of systems by adding formalism to an earlier analysis phase. This includes the higher-level language mentioned before and some aspects of data flow methodology.

COMPARISON OF DESIGN METHODOLOGIES

The diagrammatic comparison of techniques begun earlier can now be continued to include the design methodologies covered in this chapter. The stepwise refinement approaches involve procedural decomposition, and since the language form is almost English, it is placed in the upper right hand corner of the diagram (Figure 8.11). The structured analysis techniques are driven by the data flow of the problem, which is depicted in a graphical language whose format is constrained to aid in checking the consistency and completeness of the design.

Data structure techniques are exemplified by the Jackson design methodology and the approaches of Warnier and Warnier-Orr. These belong in the lower band of the diagram, along with the attempts to extend into the systems area through the use of data flow ideas. The approaches are formatted language approaches that use a combination of constrained vocabularies and graphical imagery to restrict the design (Figure 8.11).

These are not the only design approaches being suggested. Some of those not discussed here use formal languages derived from mathematical notation and Boolean logic. The reader is referred to Peters,[12] or Pressman[13] for a much broader introduction to current work.

The methodologies described in the previous sections run a very broad gamut. It seems that there are almost more approaches than there are practitioners to use them, and new approaches are being invented almost daily. What is a manager to do? Are there any compelling reasons

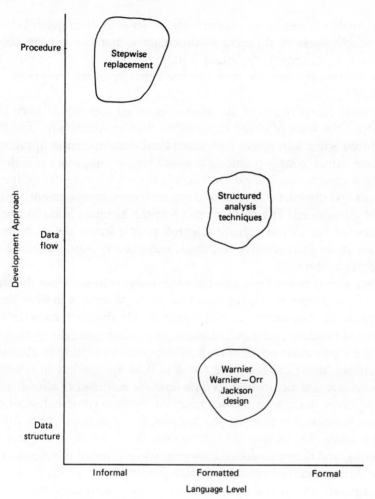

Figure 8.11. Relationship between design methodologies.

one approach should be chosen, and how do these design approaches fit into the similar spectrum that exists for planning phases? These are all very difficult questions. Obviously each of the techniques has its own users who swear that it is next to perfect in their environments. However, each also has its detractors who swear equally loudly about personal experiences that were disasters. The academic community has been unable to devise an experimental scheme to distinguish between the effectiveness of different methodologies, nor has it been able to devise a measurement system to distinguish between the empirical effects on development life cycles or the behavior of the programs after the fact.

Several comparisons of the above-described techniques have been made on the basis of observation rather than measurement, and have produced some agreement that procedural decomposition approaches are best suited to large problems in which the very approach is in doubt. When a creative designer or architect is turned loose to determine objectives and directions in a free and unconstrained environment, success is not guaranteed. The freedom given to the architect leads to circumstances where almost equally talented people given the same initial charter arrive at alternative solutions, without any way of determining the optimal choice.

Data structure methods constrain the designer most. Once the structure of the output is set, the structure of the system is to flow almost mechanically. The individuals who practice this approach have the least degree of freedom and require training in the technology. It is assumed that for a particular problem there will be little variability in approach.

Between these extremes are the data flow approaches in which an organizational structure and its data flow are assumed to already exist. The systems designer must determine an optimal combination of data processing components that will support the objectives of the organization while maintaining the information flows. Much of the freedom of procedural decomposition is present, while some of the rigors of the static data structure approach are also present.

Bergland[14] in his comparisons puts together a strategy synthesized from the extremes. The closer you are to determination of first causes, of fixing objectives, the more the procedural approaches should be used. When objectives have been set the systems analyst attempts to define problems that are small enough to be solved in a predictable fashion. For this part of the operation, data flow techniques work best. The data flow diagrams help to identify components in which the information flows are understood. Finally, once a single component has been isolated, it is time to have a programmer produce the supporting data processing structure that produces the outputs of that department, group, or division, from the inputs flowing into it.

The unifying feature that determines which approaches are best for a particular organization are the same that determine which information systems planning approach is best or what strategic planning approach is best. The character of an organization's certainty about its goals helps to determine how certain its knowledge is of the information it requires. The more certain are its information needs, the more rigorous ought its techniques to be. The less certain it is about its information requirements, the more procedurally oriented should its procedures be. Eventually, however, all approaches that try to integrate the best features of those approaches being used now should end with a data structure analysis before actual programming begins.

One of the results of academic and experimental analysis is that any discipline is better than no discipline. In this case it is better to use a technique that does not fit your organization's point of view and does not match your state of certainty about information requirements than to allow each individual to proceed independently.

REFERENCES

1. Yourdon. E., and Constantine, L., *Structured Design*, Prentice-Hall, Englewood Cliffs, NJ, 1979.
2. Myers, G., *Composite Structured Design*, Van Nostrand, New York, 1978.
3. Jackson, M., *Principles of Program Design*, Academic Press, London, 1975.
4. Jackson, M., *System Development*, Prentice-Hall, Englewood Cliffs, NJ, 1983.
5. Warnier, J. D., *Logical Construction of Programs*, Van Nostrand, New York, 1974.
6. Orr, K. T., *Structured Systems Development*, Yourdon, New York, 1977.
7. Wirth, N., "Program Development by Stepwise Refinement," *CACM*, vol. 14, no. 4, 1971, pp. 221–227.
8. McGowan, C., and Kelly, J., *Top Down Structured Programming*, Petrocelli, New York, 1975.
9. DeMarco, T., *Structured Analysis and Systems Specification*, Yourdon, New York, 1978.
10. Gane, G., and Sarson, T., *Structured Systems Analysis: Tools and Techniques*, Prentice-Hall, Englewood Cliffs, NJ, 1979.
11. Weinberg, V., *Structured Analysis*, Yourdon, New York, 1979.
12. Peters, L. J., *Software Design: Methods & Techniques*, Yourdon, New York, 1981.
13. Pressman, R. S., *Software Engineering: A Practitioner's Approach*, McGraw-Hill, New York, 1982.
14. Bergland, G. D., "A Guided Tour of Program Design Methodologie," *Computer*, vol. 14, no. 10, 1981.

QUESTIONS FOR THOUGHT

1. The game of checkers used in stepwise refinement is an example of a program emulating logical decision making. The example of the checking account reporting system used in the description of the Warnier methodology is primarily an accounting example. Try to apply each example to the other technique and conclude whether each approach is more or less suitable to one kind of problem.

2. The concept that each environment ideally attempts to optimize productivity, reliability, and manageability was introduced in this chapter. In reality all three are not equally important. For each of the methodologies described decide which of the three attributes appears most important, list the attributes in order of importance and identify those features which led you to choose the most important one for that methodology.

3. If you were in an application maintenance environment, would you use a different methodology than your colleagues who were developing applications?

4. If your organization provided an information center in which programming systems designed for professionals who use data processing were provided, and staffed the center with advisors to answer questions, would you insist that these professionals be trained in a program design methodology? Give some reasons on either side of the issue.

9

Database Concepts

DATA AS A CORPORATE RESOURCE

Enterprise Resources

One way of viewing an enterprise is to study the way that it manages its resources: the actual physical means that it possesses to generate the goods or services by which it makes a profit or otherwise justifies its existence. Typically, we have always assumed such resources to include personnel, plant, equipment, inventory, money, and so on, depending on the type of enterprise.

Ways of managing resources developed over time through increasing levels of sophistication in record keeping and decision making. Eventually, the advent of the computer age heralded advances in record keeping and in techniques for assisting people in the decision-making process. For example, raw material inventory records can be stored neatly and efficiently in a computer system. They can be cross-referenced with supplier information as well as with manufacturing process information. And they can be used by appropriate computer programs to automatically generate orders to suppliers for replenishment at the appropriate times.

Given the general and obvious nature of enterprise resources, it is perhaps difficult to imagine the birth of a new resource. But, in fact, a new resource is emerging, and that resource is *data*.

Enterprises have always possessed data: data about their history, customers, resources, competitors, and so on. The precise means for storing and maintaining that data have changed over the years, as we know. But until the most recent changes, they were geared toward producing specific results for specific problems from specific data. For example, a payroll file was maintained for a clerk or a computer program to produce paychecks every Friday. Typically, that file was used for nothing else, and if some of the data in it was needed for some other purpose, another file was created that repeated the common data. The means to manage data as a resource and to reap the benefits of doing so did not exist.

What makes the emerging interest in data as a corporate resource possible is not a change in the fundamental characteristics of data, but rather the availability of new technologies for storing and accessing that data. The new storage technology is called *database*. Improved access to the data, beyond the bounds of the database, is achieved by a wide range of data processing technology improvements, including faster components, remote terminals, and the widespread acceptance of multiuser, shared operations. Or, in other words, we can now manage data as a resource.

Why Is Data a Resource?

Data is a resource because like personnel, capital, and the other resources we have mentioned, it has a life cycle and a time value, and is sought after by the various parts of the organization. Just as it has been profitable to manage the other resources, so it is profitable to manage data, the one resource that keeps track of the others.

In the database environment that we are about to discuss, data is well managed, both in the sense of the way that it is stored on a computer system, and in the way it is tended. The database itself is managed by a data administration department (also called database administration or data resource management). While the duties of such departments vary from organization to organization, in general they have a custodial responsibility over the database which may include security, design, performance, and publicity.

As for usefulness, a database can provide much more than the simple, single files of the past. Properly organized, a database can provide:

Fast, random access to data. Examples of this would be rapid answers to customers' inquiries about orders and rapid answers to suppliers' inquiries about payments.

Access by executives to the entire range of enterprise information.

Cross-reference and matching information, such as proper matches of personnel to positions.

Automated interdepartmental functions, such as automated inventory management tied into the ordering and accounting processes.

Forecasting and projection estimates, based on history and expected factors.

Such a facility gives an enterprise a competitive advantage in terms of:

Cost reduction.

Customer goodwill.

Fewer mistakes.

Tighter executive control.

Better planning.

THE DATABASE ENVIRONMENT

Definitions

Perhaps we should begin a discussion of the database environment with another look at the question, What is data? To start to answer this rather fundamental question, we must define two words: *entity* and *attribute*.

An entity is something that an organization has a need to keep track of. Examples of entities, say, in an automobile manufacturing environment, are John Smith, assembly line worker; the automobile with serial number 135798 which just came off the assembly line; Ace Auto Parts, Inc., which is one of the company's suppliers; the sales meeting that took place three years ago in Detroit. Clearly, the concept can be expanded to include the idea of an "entity set." For example, all of the assembly line workers, all of the automobiles manufactured (this year, perhaps), all of the suppliers, all of the past sales meetings, are entity sets. Every entity has certain characteristics by which it can be described. The exact kinds of characteristics vary with the type of entity. An assembly line worker can be described by his employee number, name, address, height, weight, date of birth, skills, and so forth. An automobile can be described by its serial number, color, engine size, and options, among other qualities. Note that some attributes turn out to be unique identifiers of entities in an entity set, whereas others do not.

The traditional way of organizing data in a computer system has been through the use of fields, records, and files. Figure 9.1 shows 4 records of a personnel file. In such a file, each record represents a particular

Emp No	Name	Date of Birth	Pay Rate (Per Hour)	Dept
0010	Smith	1-5-48	5.00	7
0025	Jones	9-27-39	10.75	6
0107	Doe	8-15-52	7.82	1
0192	Adams	12-1-35	15.00	7
.				
.				
.				
.				

Figure 9.1. Personnel file.

entity (in this case, an employee). In fact, the information in each field represents the value of a particular attribute about an employee. The third employee's employee number is 0107; the forth employee's pay rate is 15.00; and so on. All of the records of the file taken together represent the entity set of employees.

Typically, organizations collect data about the various entities of concern to them, organize that data into records and files, and use that data as input to computer programs to generate whatever results are needed. The results, of course, may take the form of anything from simple lists, to random queries, to specifically computed items (such as payroll checks). Each file probably (but not always) deals with a given entity or at least with an intuitively concise area of data. Some data may be held redundantly among several files. For instance, employee department data may reside both in the payroll file and in the department organization file.

Unfortunately, as a general rule, simple files, as just described, lack six kinds of qualities that are helpful in the data processing milieu.

1. They do not encourage the enterprise's collection of data to be looked on as a unified, manageable corporate resource. This concept will be treated more fully in Chapter 10.
2. They do not encourage data storage format standardization nor employee job function specialization. It is self-evident that both of these items would improve the installation's efficiency.
3. They invite data redundancy both between different files and within individual files. (See below for further explanation.)
4. They cannot easily handle so called "multiple relationships" between data entities. (See below for further explanation.)
5. They have no inherent way of providing certain general data management functions. These include:
   a. Security.
   b. Backup and recovery.
   c. Concurrency (the problems that can arise from simultaneous updating of a record by two different users).
   d. Auditability.
6. They are poor from a data independence standpoint. That is to say, they neither discourage the practice of writing programs based closely on the structure of the data, nor do they provide a vehicle for avoiding massive program changes if the data structure must be altered in the future.

The topics of redundant data and multiple relationships deserve further discussion.

Redundant Data

The problem of redundant data can occur both within the context of one file and in the context of a collection of files. We begin the explanation by exploring the multiple file situation.

Sharing Data versus Multi-file Redundancy. An important reason for being concerned about whether data is properly managed involves the proliferation of data through the different operating units of the enterprise. It comes as no surprise that in many cases, the same piece of data is needed by several different departments to do their work. For example, a customer's address is needed by the shipping department, the billing department, the sales department, and so on. Left to their own devices, and without any higher-level planning, the individual departments will tend to generate whatever data they need to run their operations. They will do this regardless of whether the same data (possibly in combination with other data) exists in one or many other departments' files. It is a simple matter of human nature that without some specific incentive encouraging them to do otherwise, people will tend to optimize their environment for themselves. From the point of view of the individual department, it is easier, simpler from a security standpoint, and more appealing in terms of control, to have its own, private set of needed data.

The key point, though, and the point that makes this aspect of managing data imperative, is that that kind of duplication of data is *not* ideal from an overall enterprise point of view. There are three basic reasons why holding data redundantly in files in different departments (or in the same department, for that matter) is undesirable.

1.   Data held redundantly takes up that much more space on the storage devices. Depending on how the organization's data processing services are internally billed, that additional cost may be reflected in the user departments' figures or in the computer center's figures. In either case, it will be more costly to the organization as a whole.

2.   Data that is stored redundantly on several files and has to be updated, must be updated every place that it exists. It makes no sense to have different values for what should be the same data in different files. It can be argued that there are exceptions to this. As an example, inventory figures must be up-to-date for an online inventory maintenance system, but need not be exactly up-to-date for a long-term regression analysis.

The costs in this case are in processing time and record-keeping overhead. It takes that much more time to update data in several places than in one. And it takes a significant amount of effort to remember where all of the places are. An additional factor to consider is the question of who should be responsible for updating data held redundantly in several different files, when each potentially responsible person or department really cares about the data in only one of those files.

3.   Even if one were not concerned with the additional storage space and processing time that updating necessitates, there would still be the possibility of integrity problems occurring. An integrity problem is a situation in which redundant data, that should have the same value everywhere, in fact has different values in different files. The reasons for the loss of data integrity include:

Lack of knowledge about the whereabouts of all occurrences.

Poor record-keeping on the whereabouts of all occurrences.

A program error in the updating routine.

A system or hardware failure during update.

A lack of understanding about the need for consistent data.

Whatever the reason, there is then a dilemma about which of the differing values to believe is the correct one, if more than one of the values is accessed.

Data Redundancy in One File.   Assume that there is a sales organization that, of course, has to have a way of keeping track of its customers and sales representatives. Figure 9.2 shows two simple, "flat" files (many occurrences of one record type), one for the sales representatives and one for the customers. The Sales Rep file is keyed on the sales representative employee number (a unique number that can lead directly to the one record that describes a particular sales representative) and has, as one of its other fields, the sales representative's name. The Customer file is keyed on the unique customer number, and has, as one of its other fields, the employee number of the sales representative who is assigned to that account. There is one record per sales representative, recording each piece of information pertaining to him just once, and there is a like situation for each customer. This kind of data storage, said to be *nonredundant*, is set up as it should be.

If there is a requirement for finding the name of the sales representative who is identified by a particular sales representative's employee

Sales Rep No	. . .	Sales Rep Name	. . .
5		Smith	
19		Jones	
21		Doe	
.		.	
.		.	
.		.	

(a)

Figure 9.2. (a) Sales rep File.

Customer No	. . .	Sales Rep No	. . .
112		5	
215		19	
223		5	
324		5	
527		21	
632		21	
.		.	
.		.	.
.		.	

(b)

Figure 9.2. (b) Customer file.

number, a search for that sales representative's record in the Sales Rep file (Fig. 9.2a) is performed using the employee number as the key, and the name is read off. Similarly, if there is a requirement for finding the employee number of the sales representative who is responsible for a particular account, the Customer file (Fig. 9.2b) is searched for that customer's record, with the customer number serving as the key.

But what if someone wants to know the *name* of the sales representative who services a particular account, identified by customer number. That information clearly cannot be obtained from only one of the files in Figure 9.2 since the customer number information exists only in the Customer file and the sales representative *name* information exists only in the Sales Rep file. The only way to answer that question is to first look up the customer's record in the Customer file, find the employee number of the sales representative for that account, use that number to find the representative's record in the Sales Rep file, and, finally, find his or her name in that record. That kind of custom-made, multicommand, multifile access is error prone in terms of programming, expensive in terms of execution performance, and, depending on the software involved, may have to be coded separately for each such access combination.

On the other hand, if it were known in advance that such queries were going to be made, why was the data broken up into two files in the first place? If it's all contained in one file, in a meaningful way, then there are no costly multicommand, multifile accesses. Figure 9.3 shows the same data represented in one file. The sales representative (by number) is shown assigned to a particular customer, and the sales representative's name is carried in each record, as it must be in this arrangement. The two previous, simple questions that were put to the files in Figure 9.2 can still be answered. But now, in addition, the tougher, previously multifile question, What is the name of the sales representative on a particular account? can be answered with just the one file in Figure 9.3 and one command.

But there is a problem with this approach as well. In the file in Figure 9.2a, there is one record per sales representative, each containing the particulars for a given representative once. Indicating which sales representative services a particular account is simply a matter of attaching the sales representative's number to the single record that describes that customer in the file in Figure 9.2b.

But in the combined file of Figure 9.3, where all of the fundamentally different kinds of information are intermingled, the particulars of a particular sales representative must be repeated for every account that he services. A given sales representative may appear in several records in that file. It makes no sense from a logical or a retrieval standpoint to specify, for example, the sales representative name for one customer which that sales representative services and not for another. To be complete, the data must be repeated in every appropriate slot. Thus, whereas in the two files of Figure 9.2, the name "Smith" is attached to the sales representative number "5" just once, in the combined file of Figure 9.3, the name "Smith" appears with sales representative number "5" in each customer's record that Smith is responsible for.

Sales Rep No	Customer No	Sales Rep Name	. . .
5	112	Smith	
5	223	Smith	
5	324	Smith	
19	215	Jones	
21	527	Doe	
21	632	Doe	
. . .	. . .	. . .	

Figure 9.3. Combined file.

This situation causes the same set of problems that we saw in the multiple file case: increased storage, increased execution time on update, and potential integrity problems.

There appears to be a tradeoff here. In the two files of Figure 9.2, there is no redundancy (at least among the nonkey fields, strictly speaking), but a query of the type under discussion requires a multicommand, multifile access. In the combined file of Figure 9.3, the need for a multicommand, multifile access for that type of query has been eliminated, but redundancy among the nonkey fields has been introduced. Neither of those situations is tolerable for the reasons indicated above.

It would be highly desirable to have a technology that would combine the advantages of both of the above approaches. Happily, this is possible, and is one of the fundamental features of the database environment. An *integrated* data management system, a true *database* system, is one in which data can be held nonredundantly (in the sense of the files in Figure 9.2), while at the same time, a query that requires a mixture of different kinds of data (such as the query under discussion) can be specified in a single command from the highest-level programming interface. Any system that does not have that property really should not call itself a "database" system; "data management" system would be a more accurate term, in that case.

Multiple Relationships

Entities in a particular organization can relate to each other in several ways, which are described as associations and relationships.

Suppose that there is a need to store data about an organization's nonmanagement employees. Each employee is identified by a unique employee serial number. It is also desired to maintain such data as each employee's social security number, manager, and the rooms which the employee is authorized to be in. There is exactly one social security number and one manager associated with each employee, facts which are called *unary associations*. In addition to there being one social security number associated with a given employee, for a given social security number there is exactly one employee associated with it. In this case there is a unary association in each direction, and that is called a *one-to-one relationship* (Figure 9.4a).

Returning once again to employees and managers, note that although for a given employee there is only one manager, a given manager may have many employees working for him. Thus there is a unary association in one direction, and a *multiple association* in the other direction, and the combination is called a *one-to-many relationship* (Figure 9.4b).

Finally, consider the situation of employees and secure rooms. An employee may be authorized to be in several rooms, and a room will have several employees authorized to be in it. That constitutes a *many-to-many relationship* (Figure 9.4c).

The question to ask now is, How easily can data involving the two

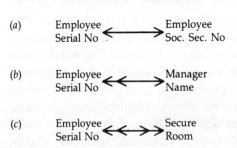

(*a*)   Employee ←——→ Employee
        Serial No   Soc. Sec. No

(*b*)   Employee ←←——→ Manager
        Serial No   Name

(*c*)   Employee ←←——→→ Secure
        Serial No   Room

Figure 9.4. Relationships. (a) One-to-One Relationship. (b) One-to-Many Relationship. (c) Many-to-Many Relationship.

kinds of associations and three kinds of relationships be stored in simple files?

In general, unary associations and one-to-one relationships are handled well by simple files. After all, a key field and a simple nonkey field in a record represent one item being attached to another item (Figure 9.5). But when multiple associations and their resulting relationships

Employee Serial No	Soc. Sec. No	Manager	. . .
1234	111-00-2222	Smith	
1572	111-22-3333	Jones	
2186	222-11-5432	Jones	
4522	522-52-5221	Smith	
4991	333-55-9999	Doe	
5283	123-45-6789	Smith	
5542	654-32-1234	Smith	
. . .	. . .	. . .	

Figure 9.5. Simple file.

are involved, simple files leave something to be desired. A multiple association can be represented "horizontally" with variable-length records (Figure 9.6a)—but this solution can cause space management and program logic problems. It can be represented "vertically" with one participant being repeated once for each of the other related participants (Figure 9.6b)—but that introduces redundancy. It can be represented with interspersed record types (Figure 9.6c)—but trying to find all occurrences of one of the record types is a problem. So none of these solutions is very good (although, when processed with certain other devices, such as indexes, relational constructs, and so on, they may well qualify as legitimate database solutions).

One of the capabilities of database management systems is the means of naturally and easily representing all of the above described types of data associations and relationships.

<table>
<tr><td>Manager</td><td colspan="4">Employee Serial Nos</td><td>. . .</td></tr>
</table>

Manager	Employee Serial Nos				. . .
Doe	4991				
Jones	1572	2186			
Smith	1234	4522	5283	5542	
.					
.					
.					

(a)

Manager	Employee Ser No	. . .
Doe	4991	
Jones	1572	
Jones	2186	
Smith	1234	
Smith	4522	
Smith	5283	
Smith	5542	
.	.	
.	.	
.	.	

(b)

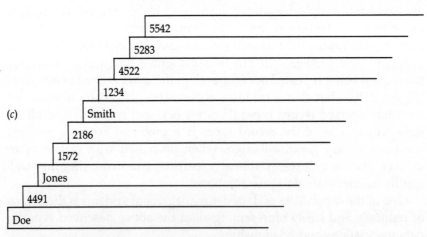

(c)

Figure 9.6. Multiple relationship representation. (a) Horizontal representation. (b) Vertical representation. (c) Interspersed records.

DATABASE MANAGEMENT SYSTEMS

Introduction

A database management system (DBMS) is a sophisticated software system that serves as an interface between application programs and query tools, and data. A true database management system (DBMS) should provide all of the facilities listed at the beginning of this chapter. At the very minimum, it must provide the capability for true integrated processing.

A DBMS consists of two major components, usually referred to as the "data description (or, definition) language" (DDL) and the "data manipulation language"(DML). The data description language is the facility that allows the users of the system to describe the form that the stored data will take when it resides in secondary storage under the control of the DBMS. The data manipulation language describes the way or ways that the data in the database can be accessed. In addition, a DBMS contains facilities for backup and recovery, concurrent processing, security, and, perhaps, auditability.

There is a very definite philosophy that pervades the database-oriented data processing environment. It revolves around separation of function, both in terms of the system's different software components and in terms of personnel.

The software component separation is what makes the data independence aspect of the database environment possible. The description of the physical storage of the data is within the bounds of the DBMS software and not in the application programs. In many cases a change to the stored structure of the data does not affect existing application programs, although this does tend to depend on the precise nature of the change.

The division of personnel is a very worthwhile, although often initially traumatic, arrangement. In a database-oriented data processing environment of medium to large size, there is a separate job function that is responsible for the database. That function, called data administration, (or sometimes database administration or data resource management), has several responsibilities, which vary from organization to organization but which can usually be divided into two categories. One of these, within the subfunction called database administration, is to manage the physical database on a day-to-day basis. Such activities can include security monitoring, backup and recovery operations, usage and performance monitoring, generating control blocks, and database software trouble shooting. The other, within the subfunction called data management, is to serve essentially as database systems analysts, or data analysts. Here the duties include planning, resolving disputes between those competing for the data resources, consulting with application development groups on database design, and organizing the use of the data dictionary.

As a result of both the software and personnel specialization, a major, nonprogramming task, which had always been the programmers' responsibility by default, is removed from them. That task, the design and maintenance of data and its structures, is now performed by an independent, specialized, expert group. Programmers can concentrate on the logic of their programs and ask the data administration organization for an interface to the data that they need.

Within the concept of a data manipulation language, there are two basic approaches:

Embedded languages.

Query languages.

In an embedded language, statements needed to access data in the database take the form of subroutine calls that are embedded within the statements of a higher-level or assembler language program. Thus a COBOL program, for example, might consist of standard COBOL logic statements, with a DML subroutine call inserted at those points in the program where the logic dictates that data from the database is needed to continue processing.

With a "query language", a user can enter commands, usually online at a terminal, to retrieve information from the database without being under the control of an application program.

It is important to note, and often not understood, that in either of the two cases, the *end user* will always, ultimately, interact with the database (in the online case) by typing simple commands into a terminal and receiving information back on the screen. This will be the case whether an application program with embedded database calls controlling the environment prompts the user for input, or whether the user is more closely controlling his own environment and is seeking ad hoc information with query language commands without being artificially prompted.

There are four basic approaches to data definition languages and their underlying data structures. All provide the ability to hold data nonredundantly, perform integrated processing, handle multiple relationships, and provide a degree of data independence. The four are:

1. The hierarchical approach.
2. The network approach.
3. The relational approach.
4. The pseudorelational or flat-file integrated approach.

The Hierarchical Approach

A prominent example of a database management system whose structure is based on the hierarchical approach is IBM's Data Language I (DL/I), which is also the database portion of its Information Management System (IMS) and Customer Information Control System (CICS).

Figure 9.7 shows two separate hierarchies, which consist of one or more record types and which are interconnected in a manner to be described. One of the hierarchies consists of DEPARTMENT, EQUIP-

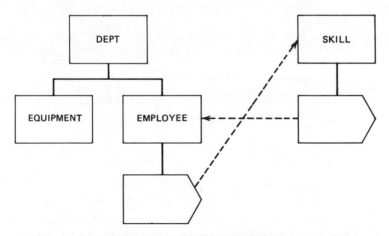

Figure 9.7. Hierarchical database.

MENT, and EMPLOYEE records; the other one consists of SKILL records. Each of these records contains several fields, naturally, which are not shown in the figure for simplicity.

A hierarchy can be described as a set of interconnected records, each of which has precisely one "parent" record type, except for the "root" (at the top of the hierarchy) which has none. In Figure 9.7 DEPARTMENT is the root and is the parent of EQUIPMENT and EMPLOYEE. In turn, EQUIPMENT and EMPLOYEE can be described as "children" of DEPARTMENT. The lines connecting the various records are called "branches." A key concept in the use of the hierarchy as the basic structural form in DL/I is that every branch represents a one-to-many relationship. Thus, Figure 9.7 indicates that each department has several pieces of equipment assigned to it and has several employees working in it. A given piece of equipment and a given employee are each associated with only one department. Figure 9.8 shows a "database record," that is, a single occurrence of the DEPARTMENT root, together with all of its dependent occurrences. A typical way to physically store such an arrangement is with a combination of types of pointers. For example, there can be a "child pointer" connecting the finance department to employee Adams, and there can be "twin pointers" connecting all of the employees of the finance department together in what is called a "twin chain."

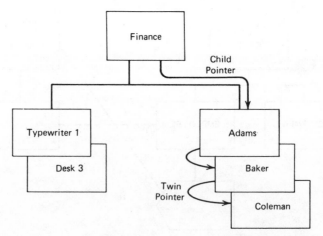

Figure 9.8. A hierarchical occurrence of the DEPARTMENT database.

A hierarchy cannot directly represent a many-to-many relationship, but two one-to-many relationships connected to an additional segment can. Notice that the single segment type or "root only" database SKILL is connected to the EMPLOYEE segment of the DEPARTMENT database by two additional segments. Such an interconnection is called a "logical relationship" and the two additional segments are called "logical child" segments. The interconnection is physically accomplished with several additional pointers. Using this arrangement the system can keep track of all of the skills that a particular employee has, and all of the employees who have a particular skill. In fact, additional information pertaining to the relationship between an employee and a skill (such as how many years the employee has had the skill) can be stored in the logical child segments connecting them. Such information is called "intersection data."

Access to the data in a hierarchy is through the root segment. When a key field is chosen, a given root occurrence can be found either through an index based on the key or through a random-access method based on the key. Subordinate segments are then located by the DL/I software following the pointers. Additional indexed access to any field in any segment can be had with the use of a "secondary index."

Notice, as regards redundancy, that the department information is stored only once, regardless of how many employees are in it or how many pieces of equipment it has assigned to it. Also, with the knowledge that an employee can only be assigned to one department, employee information is stored only once per employee, regardless of how many skills the employee has, while at the same time the skill information is stored only once per skill, regardless of how many employees have it. Thus the hierarchical arrangement is capable of maintaining one-to-many and many-to-many arrangements, and is capable of holding data in a nonredundant form.

The two hierarchies in Figure 9.7 are known as "physical databases." They describe data in the way that it is stored on the physical storage media. Figure 9.9 shows a "logical database." A logical database consists of a subset of the segment types of a physical database (or of several physical databases connected by logical relationships). Its root segment must either be the root of a physical hierarchy or a segment that is pointed to by a secondary index. Actually, the embodiment of a logical database does not involve any duplication of the physical data, but

Figure 9.9. Logical hierarchy.

rather is created using control blocks that map onto the physical data. Programmers base their programs on the logical database structures. Thus, using the logical hierarchy in Figure 9.9, a programmer could find information about a skill of a single employee in a given department without necessarily being aware that the physical data resides in two separate physical databases. In fact, the programmer can make such an access with one call from the high-level programming interface.

This programming capability indicates that the data structure permits integration of data, as previously described in this section. In addition, there is a great deal of data independence since in many cases the structure itself can be modified without affecting existing programs.

The Network Approach

Several database management systems are based on a network approach commonly known as the "CODASYL" approach. CODASYL is the Conference on Data Systems Languages, "an organization composed of volunteer representatives of computer manufacturers and users in industry and the Federal Governments of Canada and the United States of America" (CODASYL 1978 Specifications). CODASYL's Data Base Task Group (DBTG) has published, and updated several times, a set of specifications for a database management system, subsets of which have been implemented by several companies. These systems include Cullinet's IDMS, Univac's DMS 1100, and Digital Equipment's DBMS-10, among others. Another system that has network aspects but that is not as close as the others to the CODASYL specifications is Cincom's Total.

A network is essentially an unrestricted set of nodes (record types in this case) and connecting branches or edges. In fact, a hierarchy is merely a particular type of network. In the DL/I terminology of the last section, a network has no concept of a "root" node, and records may have several parent record types as well as several child record types. Thus, the two hierarchies of Figure 9.7 are legitimate networks, as is the structure shown in Figure 9.10. Using a single-headed arrow to represent a unary association and a double-headed arrow to represent a multiple association, Figure 9.10 indicates that a department has several employees and several offices, and each office has several employees housed in it. There is no sense of "root", and it can be argued that the EMPLOYEE record has two "parents."

Fundamentally, the network approach to database management systems shares many similarities with the hierarchical approach. The record occurrences are interconnected by pointers; the branches represent one-to-many relationships; special records called "link" records are used with two one-to-many relationships to implement many-to-many relationships; and there is a sense of physical versus logical structures (called "schemas" and "subschemas"). The records in the network are "integrated" in the same sense that hierarchical records are integrated.

There are some differences as well. Two connected record types form a "set," and some of the processing manipulations are based on the set concept. The occurrences of any record type can, if desired, be accessed on a random or direct basis. The pointer collection is a bit different, as is the way that a programmer views and programs with the structure.

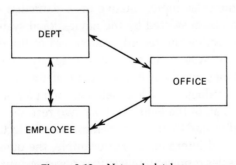

Figure 9.10. Network database.

It is important to note that both the hierarchical and network systems are called "navigational systems" since in both cases programmers must traverse a preconnected (preintegrated) set of records. It has usually been felt that this preconnection is a benefit in terms of performance but is restrictive in terms of the complexity of the design process and later modifications to the design.

The Relational Approach

The relational approach to database management is a significant departure from the two preceding navigational systems in several ways. The key point is that the files, which are substantially simple, linear files (of the type in Figure 9.2) are, at least in theory, unconnected by artificial means such as pointers. The capability for integrated processing is there, but the integration is performed *at the time the query is made through the power of the software*, and not in advance through the power of the data structure, as in the navigational systems.

In Figure 9.2, the two files are simple, unconnected files, with no redundancy among the nonkey fields, as was pointed out earlier. Significantly, though, each of the two files has a "join" field that shares a common domain of values: Sales Rep No. (the field names happen to be identical in this case too, but that is incidental). In fact, comparing values of the join fields is the vehicle with which a relational system performs integration. That the two files were designed in the first place so that the join fields happen to appear in the correct places is a result of a process called "data normalization," which will be discussed in Chapter 10.

The earlier discussion of Figure 9.2 posed the integrated query, "What is the *name* of the sales representative on a particular account?" This kind of query can be answered by the navigational systems because of the pointers connecting the record occurrences of the different record types. A relational system, in the worst case, dynamically compares every record of one file with every record of the other file, seeking matches between values of the join fields in each pair of records. When a match is found, all of the fields of those two records are entered into a newly created file, and then other operators can "select" and "project" out only the needed information. For example, the question, "What is the name of the sales representative who services account number 324?"

would be satisfied by the system's joining the two files of Figure 9.2 with Sales Rep No. as the join field in each of the files. The resultant file would include a record that would bring together the values "5," "Smith," and "324." Subsequent appropriate operations would select that particular record from the file, and project "Smith" from that record as the answer.

The freedom of being able to perform integrated processing on physically unconnected files is very enticing. Database design is greatly simplified and data independence is improved with the relational approach. The inevitable question, then, of why the early history and current state of database management systems have been monopolized by the navigational systems can be answered in one word: performance. Clearly, performing a full, worst-case join, as above, on large files, is prohibitive in terms of time.

More recently, several organizations have pursued two main approaches, hardware and software, to try to overcome this problem, although much work in the area remains. Relational Software's Oracle, IBM's SQL and Query by Example, and Relational Technology's Ingres, for example, are all based on the software approach. The techniques involved include large-scale use of indices for faster access to more fields, some low-level interconnection of files, and a query preprocessor that attempts to find the most efficient way to answer a query before accessing the database. The question in the example above, for instance, could have been answered without a full-scale join if the software could have figured out that only one record in the Customer file (and then one record in the Sales Rep file) was involved.

The hardware approach involves parallel technology and the realization that if it takes a certain length of time to do a join comparing 2 records at a time, then it takes significantly less time if, say, 10 comparisons can be done simultaneously.

The Pseudorelational or Flat-File Integrated Approach

Finally, there is a fourth, hybrid approach to DBMS structure, which has been loosely called "pseudorelational" or "flat-file integrated." The files are physically unconnected flat files, like the relational approach, but the actual integration of the data must be done in advance of the query, like the navigational approach. In Software A. G.'s ADABAS and

Computer Corporation of America's Model 204, integration is accomplished by the construction of an additional file, which is really a long list of which records of one particular file have a match in a certain join field with another particular file. In IBM's System/38, an index in the form of a particular kind of tree is created that involves the concatenation of the keys of, say, a master file and a transaction file so that all of the transactions that refer to a given master can be associated with it.

THE TOOLS OF DATA MANAGEMENT

Beyond the database management system, there are a number of other software tools used in data management.

Data Dictionary

A data dictionary is a set of interrelated files that describe the entities of the data processing environment itself. Such entities include files, records, fields, DP personnel, reports, control blocks, computer hardware, and so forth.

An easy way to understand the concept of data dictionaires is to compare them to other collections of files. Figure 9.11 shows two typical files: the payroll department's personnel file and the manufacturing department's parts inventory file. Each file's purpose, in a sense, is to help the respective department managers manage their affairs in an efficient manner. The payroll file has one record per employee, each containing the data required to do that employee's payroll processing, and a similar statement can be made about the inventory file. The question to be asked is, What information should be stored about the data processing environment itself to allow data processing managers to more efficiently manage it? As previously mentioned, the entities of importance to the data processing environment include fields, files, reports, and so on.

Figure 9.12 shows part of a data dictionary. Specifically it shows the fields file and the files file. Just as employees constitute a manageable entity of the personnel department, and parts a manageable entity of the manufacturing department, so fields and files are manageable en-

Employee Number	Employee Name	Home City	...
101	Smith	NYC	
123	Jones	NYC	
158	Doe	Chi	

Payroll File

Part Number	Part Name	QOH	...
1044	Nut	2000	
1726	Bolt	3000	
2100	Screw	1000	

Inventory File

Figure 9.11. Two typical DP Files.

Field Name	Field Type	Field Length	...
Emp. No	N	3	
Emp. Nm.	A	15	
Home City	A	15	
Part No.	N	4	
Part Nm.	A	20	
QOH	N	5	

Fields File

File Name	No. of Records	Prod. Status	...
Payroll	200	P	
Inventy	700	P	

Files File

Figure 9.12. A portion of a data dictionary.

tities of the data processing department. In Figure 9.12, the fields file records information about the fields of the two files of figure 9.11, and the files file records information about the two files of Figure 9.11. Another facet of data dictionaries, which is not shown in Figure 9.12, is their ability to cross-reference the data among their files. Thus, not only can a data dictionary store data about fields and about files, but it can also record, for example, which fields appear in which files.

The role of the data dictionary has been steadily expanding beyond that of simply a documentation device for data processing managers. In terms of the subject matter of this book, data dictionaries are increasingly being considered a tool in both detailed systems analysis and database design. Systems analysts can use the data dictionary to find out whether data needed for the new system under study exists in a system already in operation in the installation. In fact, since systems analysts are the first people to come in contact with the proposed fields of a new system, it is argued that they should have the responsibility to input much of the (nonphysical) data about the fields of the new system. By the time the database design step is reached, the database designers will find the set of fields (and possibly the relationships among the fields) neatly stored in the data dictionary and ready for input to the database design step.

Query Packages and Report Writers

Earlier, we stated that the two major types of access to the database are through a query language, or through statements embedded in the flow of a host language. It should, in addition, be noted that various software vendors have devised query packages for specific database management systems which normally work only on an embedded basis.

A great deal of output involving the data in databases involves a relatively small amount of computation, but a relatively high amount of repetitiveness and volume. Such output ranges from simple bookkeeping tasks such as generating payroll checks and generating accounts receivables listings, to straightforward lists of the data in the database. For such applications, a range of software tools, which have come to be known as report writers, has been developed. These tools are limited in scope compared to the general nature of higher-level language code, but are quite efficient in generating reports quickly and easily.

On-Line Application Generators

Whereas report writers are helpful in the generation of simple, printed output, on-line application generators are useful in producing on-line, interactive applications. As with report writers, these tools are limited in the complexity of the applications that they can handle, but are very fast and efficient in allowing simple on-line, interactive applications to be written.

The use of these types of programming and database tools is expanding rapidly, as their design becomes more efficient. It has been suggested by many that future programming will increasingly be accomplished through the use of techniques of this type. It should also be noted that those who wish to gain the advantages of accelerated application development for reports, queries, and simple online applications *must* first invest in a DBMS.

BIBLIOGRAPHY

Date, C. J., *An Introduction to Database Systems*, 3d ed., Addison-Wesley, Reading, MA, 1981.

King, J. M., *Evaluating Data Base Management Systems*, Van Nostrand Reinhold, New York, 1981.

Kroenke, D., *Database: A Professional's Primer*, Science Research Associates, Chicago, 1978.

Martin, J., *Computer Data-Base Organization*, 2d ed., Prentice-Hall, Englewood Cliffs, NJ, 1977.

Ross, R. G., *Data Base Systems: Design, Implementation, and Management*, AMACOM, New York, 1978.

QUESTIONS FOR THOUGHT

1. Statement: "Database management systems today are, for the most part, complex pieces of software which can be run on a variety of hardware systems, using a variety of operating systems. In the future, the concept of database will be an integral, embedded feature of new computer systems." Do you agree or disagree with that statement? Defend your position.

2. Of all of the advantages of the database approach, which do you feel is the most important? The least important? Why?

3. Many people believe that the functional center of the database environment of the future will be a sophisticated, active data dictionary, which will aid in documentation, management, and automated, on-line control. Elaborate on what that environment might look like and how it might operate.

10

Database Design

INTRODUCTION

Database design refers to the process of arranging the data fields needed by one or more applications into an organized structure. That structure must foster the required relationships among the fields while conforming to the physical constraints of the particular database management system in use. There are really two parts to the process. There is "logical" database design, which is then followed by "physical" database design. There are several techniques for performing logical database design, each with its own emphasis and approach. Physical database design is a function of the database management system for which the database is being designed.

Logical database design is an implementation-independent exercise that is performed on the fields and relationships needed for one or more (possibly many) applications. The fields are grouped together and, based on the type of DBMS to be used, the groups are appropriately interconnected. Regardless of which of the several logical database design techniques is used, the end result is that each group of fields forms a naturally related set of data. A word of caution: The term *conceptual database design*, which has at times been used in the literature synonymously with logical database design and at other times to mean other intermediate stages of design, will not be used in this text.

Physical database design is an implementation-dependent exercise that takes the results of logical database design and further refines them according to the characteristics of the particular database management system in use. Usually the groupings of fields are maintained, although controlled alterations can be made. Other decisions, such as access methods and supplementary index usage are made at this point. These matters will be discussed in more detail later.

THE NEED FOR DATABASE DESIGN

A variety of reasons make careful database design essential. These include data redundancy, application performance, data independence, data security, and ease of programming. All are important factors in the data processing environment, and all can be adversely affected by a poor database design.

Intrafile and Multifile Redundancy

Proper database design is essential to avoid both the intrafile and multifile redundancies discussed earlier. Strictly speaking, the amount of apparent redundancy (key and nonkey fields) varies with the type of database management system for which the files are being designed. In all cases, the goal, at least in the early stages of design, is to eliminate all redundancy among the nonkey fields. In the later stages of design, as the data takes on the form of the structures of the particular database management system, there may or may not be overt redundancy among the key fields. Specifically, the relational approach requires certain fields to appear as attributes of different relations, whereas in the navigational method, field duplication is replaced by pointers.

Performance

Performance—the operational speed of applications and systems—can be affected or influenced by a number of factors in the database environment. Several of these factors are common data processing issues that are beyond the control of database design, such as CPU processing speed, disk data transfer rate, channel speed, the contention of different applications sharing the same hardware system, and, of course, the efficiency of the techniques embodied in the database management system itself.

However, there are many elements of the database environment affecting performance that are under the control of the database designer. Many of them are product specific; that is they depend on quirks of the particular database management system. But others are general enough in nature to deserve mention here and further discussion later. Most of them are directly or indirectly related to the scourge of database performance: the number and nature of accesses to the data on the random-access, secondary storage devices, commonly known as "disk I/Os."

One common example of a performance-related choice is which access method to use and exactly how to implement it for the application at hand. The designer may have to decide whether to use a direct-access method or an indexed method, how many fields to index, which data placement or "hashing" method to use (in the direct case), and so on. There may be a variety of types of pointers to link various records together, each with different performance ramifications for different types of applications. There may be a variety of ways to design the juxtaposition of various record types in a hierarchy or network, and, in addition, options for grouping occurrences on the same direct-access device. Further comments on specific systems will be made later.

Data Independence

Data independence, the ability to modify data structures without affecting existing programs, is fundamentally a function of the data model used by a particular database management system. All such systems provide an enhanced degree of data independence when compared to ordinary file processing. Nevertheless, there are database design choices that can be made, particularly when dealing with hierarchical and network DBMSs, which can affect the degree of independence achieved. The intricacy of the matter does not even end there, because beyond the specifics of the data structure and of the database design, the way that a program is written can affect data independence.

Data Security

Database management systems generally have a variety of built-in data security safeguards. These range from passwords associated with a given user, to passwords associated with particular data, to various ways of prohibiting all but certain users to perform certain operations on certain data. Data security becomes an issue in database design when the minimum amount of data that the system is capable of returning from the database on a program call is greater than the amount that the person who executed that program has the right to see. In that case, the structure may have to be designed so that data, which otherwise would have been placed together into a retrievable unit, is split over several units.

Ease of Programming

While the use of database management systems requires programmers to learn new concepts and protocols, the overall effect of the use of DBMSs is to decrease programming complexity and the attendant programming error rates. One reason for that is the standardization that results from using the same protocol for data manipulations in all programs. Another reason involves the integrated nature of the data structures, which allows a programmer to obtain data from physically separate files or distinct record types (depending on the data model used) with one call from the high-level programming interface. Without the use of a DBMS, and assuming the avoidance of unacceptable levels of data redundancy, the alternative would be accessing data in one file, using it to access data in another file, and so on through as many files as necessary to satisfy the query. This procedure is clearly much more error prone, not to mention more time consuming to write, than those associated with DBMS.

Within the improved level of programming that the use of database management systems affords, certain decisions in database design can make the programmer's job somewhat harder or easier. Unfortunately, the decisions that can simplify programming specifications usually have an adverse affect on data redundancy, system performance, or both. For example, combining fields together within one data structure unit may allow a programmer to simplify the specifications needed to retrieve that data, but will usually result in an increase in data redundancy. Adding additional indices into the data structure creates more flexibility in online retrieval and simplifies program retrieval specifications, at the expense of performance when the data must be updated. A highly volatile file with a large number of indices connected to it may degrade the performance of the entire system.

DATABASE DESIGN METHODOLOGIES

This section will present two of the most common database design techniques. In both cases we will begin with the data-oriented information generated as output from systems analysis, and proceed to relational, pseudorelational, hierarchical, and network database models. The method of explanation will be by example, with appropriate commentary along the way.

The first method, "data normalization and data structuring," is representative of the class of methods that take as input a list of fields and the associations among those fields. The second method, the "entity-relationship" method, is representative of the class of methods that take entities and relationships as input.[1]

Data Normalization and Data Structuring

The Example. This first method of database design requires one major step for the relational approach and two major steps for the other three approaches. Fortunately, for the convenience of explanation, the one major step for the relational approach is, in fact, the first of the two steps for the other three approaches.

Figure 10.1 shows an example set of fields that concern the personnel information system of a nationwide chain of automobile repair shops. It is clear from the list of fields that the goal of the system is to keep track of the company's mechanics, their skills, locations, and other associated information. The Mechanic's Skill Proficiency Level field is intended to store a particular mechanic's proficiency level in a particular skill. (It is worth taking an aside here to note that this set of fields was chosen for this example to make certain database design points. As we shall see, a much higher percentage of the fields in this collection will participate as key fields than would be the case in most actual situations.)

Mechanic Number (Mech No)
Skill Number (Skll No)
Skill Category (Skll Cat)
Mechanic Name (Mech Name)
Mechanic Home Phone (Mech Phn)
Shop Number (Shop No)
Shop City
Shop Supervisor (Supv)
Mechanic's Skill Proficiency Level (Prof)

Figure 10.1. Example set of fields.

Figure 10.2 shows the associations among our example fields. The single-headed arrows indicate unique identifications. Thus association 2 indicates that for a given mechanic number, there is exactly one name associated with it (mechanic numbers are unique), and association 10 indicates that for a given shop number, there is exactly one city associated with it. If I give you *mechanic 81*, you can uniquely give me back

---

1. Mech No $\longrightarrow\!\!\!\!\longrightarrow$ Skll No
2. Mech No $\longrightarrow$ Mech Name
3. Mech No $\longrightarrow$ Mech Phn
4. Mech No $\longrightarrow$ Shop No
5. Mech No $\longrightarrow$ Supv
6. Skll No $\longrightarrow\!\!\!\!\longrightarrow$ Mech No
7. Skll No $\longrightarrow$ Skll Cat
8. Shop No $\longrightarrow\!\!\!\!\longrightarrow$ Mech No
9. Shop No $\longrightarrow$ Supv
10. Shop No $\longrightarrow$ Shop City
11. Mech No, Skll No $\longrightarrow$ Prof

Figure 10.2. Associations between the fields.

John Smith. If I give you *shop 12*, you can uniquely give me back *Chicago.* Note that unless explicitly stated, the inverse cannot be assumed to hold true. Thus there may be several John Smiths in the company, and there may be several shops in Chicago. The double-headed arrows in Figure 10.2 indicate multiple associations: An instance of the item on the left may be associated with several instances of the item on the right. Association 1 says that a mechanic may have several skills. Association 8 says that a shop may have several mechanics working in it.

Potential Database Problems. Before beginning the database design process, it is instructive to revisit the problems that poor database design can cause, in the context of this example. Figure 10.3 shows seven sample records of a file made up of all of the fields listed in Figure 10.1. It assumes that no database design effort was made, and thus all of the fields were just lumped together in one file. Mechanic number and skill number were chosen as a compound (multifield) key since the two taken together can uniquely identify a record in the file. Note that it follows that since a key value can uniquely identify a record in a file, the key value uniquely determines the values of the nonkey fields of that record (conversely the nonkey values are "dependent" on the key value).

It is evident that there is a great deal of redundancy in the file in Figure 10.3. Mechanic 35 has 3 skills. To represent that requires 3 records, since mechanic number and skill number must be taken together to form a legitimate key. In fact, each mechanic number–skill number pair must appear in a separate record in order to be associated with a proficiency level number, which is dependent on the combination of

Mech No	Skll No	Skll Cat	Mech Nm	Mech Age	Shop No	Shop City	Supv	Prof
21	113	Body	Adams	55	52	NYC	Brown	3
35	113	Body	Baker	32	44	LA	Green	5
35	179	Engn	Baker	32	44	LA	Green	1
35	204	Tran	Baker	32	44	LA	Green	6
50	179	Engn	Cody	40	44	LA	Green	2
77	148	Tire	Doe	47	52	NYC	Brown	6
77	361	Engn	Doe	47	52	NYC	Brown	6

Key spans over Mech No and Skll No columns.

Figure 10.3. Sample records.

who the mechanic is and what skill is under discussion. One example of redundancy, as a result of this situation, is that the mechanic's age, name, shop number, shop city, and supervisor, must be carried in the file as many times as the number of skills that the mechanic has. Another example is that the information about who the supervisor is at a particular shop must be carried at least once for each mechanic who works at that shop. These facts bring with them all of the standard problems of redundancy: extra storage space, extra time spent on update, and potential integrity problems.

Another potential problem with this file involves the deletion and addition of data. Suppose that Adams and Doe are the only two mechanics in shop 52. If they quit, and, as might reasonably be expected, we delete the records concerning them, then we have also deleted from the file the fact that Brown is the supervisor of shop 52. Those two fundamentally different pieces of information cannot exist separately in the current design. A similar, but reversed, situation exists in adding data to the file. Ordinarily, if we add a new mechanic to the file we would expect to find the shop city and supervisor information from records already in the file that involve that shop. But if the new mechanic is the first one in the shop, then the shop city and supervisor data doesn't currently exist in the file and must be sought elsewhere. Adding a mechanic who does not yet possess any skills could have serious implications in terms of the key.

Thus it is clear that simply putting all of the fields into one file leaves a great deal to be desired.

Data Normalization. Data normalization is a methodology for arranging fields into tables (or files, or relations) so that redundancy among the nonkey fields is eliminated. Each of the resultant tables deals with a single area of knowledge, as opposed to the mixture seen in Figure 10.3. The input required by the normalization process is a list of the set of data fields and the associations among them, as, for instance, in Figures 10.1 and 10.2. Nevertheless, it is easier to explain the process in the context of an example that includes sample records, and so we shall continue with the example that we have been using. We stress again that the lists of data fields and associations, which are the required inputs here, are parts of the output of the systems analysis phase.

Unnormalized Data. Figure 10.4 shows the example data in a somewhat loosely structured arrangement called "unnormalized" form. Unnormalized data may include such situations as a multivalued field. For instance, the second record in Figure 10.4 refers to mechanic 35, and

Mech No	Skll No	Skll Cat	Mech Nm	Mech Age	Shop No	Shop City	Supv	Prof
21	113	Body	Adams	55	52	NYC	Brown	3
35	113	Body	Baker	32	44	LA	Green	5
	179	Engn						1
	204	Tran						6
50	179	Engn	Cody	40	44	LA	Green	2
70	148	Tire	Doe	47	52	NYC	Brown	6
	361	Engn						6

Figure 10.4. Unnormalized data.

notes, within that single record, that he has 3 skills. This form of data has certain distinct disadvantages, including the need for some form of variable-length records, and additional complexity for the programmer that would invariably lead to increased programming errors. Furthermore, in the case of mechanic 35's record, we happen to know that skill 113 matches up with the skill category "body," and so on through all of the listed pairs of skill numbers and categories, but such matches may not always exist in all similar situations, which would cause incredible confusion.

First Normal Form.   First normal form data has the property that every data entry, or field value, must be nondecomposable. Figure 10.5 is the first normal form representation of the data in Figure 10.4. Every field entry of every record consists of only one piece of nonsubdividable data. Essentially, the unnormalized records with multivalued fields were cloned to produce several records, with some data repeated, as necessary. Except for the fact that the data shown in Figure 10.3 is meant to represent only part of a file, while the data in Figure 10.5 is meant to represent an entire file (for illustrative purposes), the two are identical. Clearly, the first normal form representation of data is not, in and of itself, helpful as a redundancy-controlling arrangement, but is merely a jumping-off point for further work.

Second Normal Form.   We have already established that the data in Figure 10.5 (like Figure 10.3) is highly redundant. At this point the

Mech No	Skll No	Skll Cat	Mech Nm	Mech Age	Shop No	Shop City	Supv	Prof
21	113	Body	Adams	55	52	NYC	Brown	3
35	113	Body	Baker	32	44	LA	Green	5
35	179	Engn	Baker	32	44	LA	Green	1
35	204	Tran	Baker	32	44	LA	Green	6
50	179	Engn	Cody	40	44	LA	Green	2
77	148	Tire	Doe	47	52	NYC	Brown	6
77	361	Engn	Doe	47	52	NYC	Brown	6

(Columns "Mech No" and "Skll No" are grouped under the label "Key")

Figure 10.5.   First normal form.

methodology turns to the question of what to look for and change in the data structure to begin to alleviate the redundancy.

The fact that the mechanic number–skill number combination of fields is a valid key for this file has already been established. Again, this means, among other things, that every nonkey field in the file is dependent on the key, which can be verified by the single-arrow associations in Figure 10.2. Although both parts of that compound key are necessary to define the proficiency field (association 11 in Figure 10.2), only one or the other of the two parts of the key are needed to define each of the other nonkey fields. This fact is a clue to the redundancy and its at least partial elimination.

Figure 10.6 shows the same data in second normal form. It has been divided into 3 tables, each of which has the property that its entire key is needed to define each of its nonkey fields. Within a given table, no nonkey field is defined by part of the key alone. Several fields were duplicated in this process. Mechanic number, which, of course, appeared only once as a field in first normal form, now appears both in the Mechanic Table and in the Proficiency Table. As we shall see, that kind of field duplication is necessary, at this stage (and for the relational case in general) among those fields participating as key fields. In fact, though, the total number of field value occurrences has decreased from 63 in Figure 10.5 to 55 in Figure 10.6, indicating a net decrease in redundancy. Also notice that individually identifiable areas of knowledge are represented in each of the tables (although not to the final degree, as we shall soon see).

Third Normal Form. The Skill Table and the Proficiency Table in Figure 10.6 are both completely free of nonkey redundancy at this point. In fact, they are both already in third normal form. But a glance at the Mechanic Table will reveal some residual redundancy. For example, both records 1 and 4 indicate that shop 52 is in New York City and is supervised by Brown; likewise for records 2 and 3 and shop 44. Yet, according to the list of relationships, the key of that table—mechanic number—identifies each of its other fields, and, since the key consists of only one field, the second normal form rule of nonkey dependence on the entire key is, of course, met.

The problem has to do with the relationships between shop number and shop city, and between shop number and supervisor (relationships 9 and 10 in Figure 10.2). Shop number defines shop city and supervisor,

Mech No	Mech Nm	Mech Age	Shop No	Shop City	Supv
21	Adams	55	52	NYC	Brown
35	Baker	32	44	LA	Green
50	Cody	40	44	LA	Green
77	Doe	47	52	NYC	Brown

(*a*) Mechanic Table

Key

Skll No	Skll Cat
113	Body
148	Tire
179	Engn
204	Tran
361	Engn

(*b*) Skill Table

Key

Mech No	Skll No	Prof
21	113	3
35	113	5
35	179	1
35	204	6
50	179	2
77	148	6
77	361	6

(*c*) Proficiency Table

Figure 10.6. Second normal form.

but is clearly not a valid key of the entire table (it does not define mechanic number, mechanic name, or mechanic age). Thus the situation is one of a nonkey field defining other nonkey fields. This kind of incestuous relationship, which is another kind of indication of fundamentally different kinds of information being mixed together in the same table, is what is causing the remaining redundancy.

Figure 10.7 shows the third normal form representation of the data. Notice that a new table, the Shop Table, has been created to separate out the shop-related data. Also notice that in splitting off the Shop Table, a copy of the shop number column was left behind in the Mechanic Table. That is because that was the only way to continue to indicate which shop a mechanic is associated with.

So, in third normal form we can say that in each table, no situation exists where a nonkey field defines another nonkey field. There is a fairly common exception to this when there are two fields that *could* be the key, such as an employee identification number and a social security number. The one of the two that is not chosen as the key would seem to be a nonkey field that then defines other nonkey fields, but in this specific case it is not a violation of the stated rule.

The third normal form data in Figure 10.7 contains no redundancy among the nonkey fields. That is the goal that we sought.

Other Normal Forms. As further research continues to be done in this field, new problems and solutions arise. Two exceptional situations have been identified that involve third normal form data, which still contain redundancy. Both involve combinations of multiple associations. They have been named fourth and fifth normal forms, are encountered infrequently in practice, and are beyond the scope of this book.

The Value of Normalized Tables. Two major statements can be made about normalized data. One is that this form of data, free of redundancy among the nonkey fields, is an intermediate plateau in the design of data structures for hierarchical and network databases.

The other point is that normalized data, subject to possible structural modifications for performance reasons, *is* the final design for relational databases. In fact, the normalization process assures that join fields will appear in all of the tables that they should appear in based on the given relationships among the fields. That is a very strong statement and a

Key

{Mech No}

Mech No	Mech Name	Mech Age	Shop No
21	Adams	55	52
35	Baker	32	44
50	Cody	40	44
77	Doe	47	52

(a) Mechanic Table

Key

{Skill No}

Skill No	Skill Cat
113	Body
148	Tire
179	Engn
204	Tran
361	Engn

(b) Skill Table

Key

{Mech No, Skill No}

Mech No	Skill No	Prof
21	113	3
35	113	5
35	179	1
35	204	6
50	179	2
77	148	6
77	361	6

(c) Proficiency Table

Key

{Shop No}

Shop No	Shop City	Supv.
44	LA	Green
52	NYC	Brown

(d) Shop Table

Figure 10.7. Third normal form.

fact central to the use of normalization for the design of all of the types of databases.

The same remarks about normalization producing the database design, subject to performance modifications, applies to pseudorelational databases, subject to the addition of tables, or indexes, that prejoin the normalized tables based on the data relationships and application needs. In fact, the same basic remark also applies to ordinary, nondatabase, flat files, for which normalization is also an ideal design technique.

Data Structuring—Hierarchical Databases. Generally, in converting from a set of normalized tables to a hierarchical data structure, the normalized tables are transformed into nodes in the hierarchy. Occurrences of the same and different record types are connected by a variety of types of pointers. In effect, certain of the normalized tables are chosen to have their records prejoined to each other to physically realize a selected set of relationships. The primary advantage of this technique is superior performance during execution of accesses based on those relationships.

The procedure for designing a hierarchical database, such as for a DL/I system, begins with a set of normalized tables. We will continue following the example we have been using and resume with the normalized tables in Figure 10.7.

The Structuring Process. The process begins by noting the multiple associations in Figure 10.2, the original list of associations among the fields. A multiple association whose inverse multiple association does not appear on the list is recorded as a one-to-many relationship. There is one such relationship in Figure 10.2:

Shop No $\longrightarrow\!\!\!\!\longrightarrow$ Mech No

which is association 8. A multiple association whose inverse does appear on the list is recorded as a many-to-many relationship. There is one such relationship in Figure 10.2:

Mech No $\longleftarrow\!\!\!\!\longrightarrow$ Skill No

which is formed by the combination of associations 1 and 6.

Next, form hierarchies from the one-to-many relationships. Since every branch of a hierarchical data structure represents a one-to-many relationship, this step is quite straightforward. Figure 10.8 shows a hierarchy built out of the 1 one-to-many relationship in the example. The mechanic and shop nodes in the hierarchy are directly derived from the normalized mechanic and shop tables of Figure 10.7. Note that the SHOP NO. field in the mechanic table in Figure 10.7 does not appear in the mechanic record in Figure 10.8. In the normalized tables, the only way to indicate which shop a mechanic works at is to include SHOP NO. as a field in the mechanic table. The fact that SHOP NO. also appears as a field in the shop table seems, in a sense, to be a form of redundancy involving a field that serves, as least in one table, as the key. But when those tables are converted into records in a hierarchy, which represents the one-to-many relationship between shops and mechanics, the SHOP NO. field is not included in the mechanic record. The point is that the knowledge of which shop a mechanic works at is now stored by means of the pointers that connect a particular shop to all of the mechanics who work there.

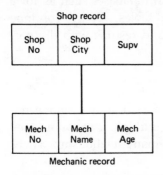

Figure 10.8. Hierarchy representing the one-to-many relationship.

A many-to-many relationship cannot be built directly in a hierarchical data structure. It must be simulated by 2 one-to-many relationships, each of whose targets, or "many" side record types is the same, specially created new record. When the data is eventually loaded using this structure, there will be one occurrence of the new special record *for every occurrence of the relationship* (for every connection between two entities in the relationship). Figure 10.9 shows the hierarchy of Figure 10.8 on the left, with a new (single-record type) hierarchy on the right, consisting

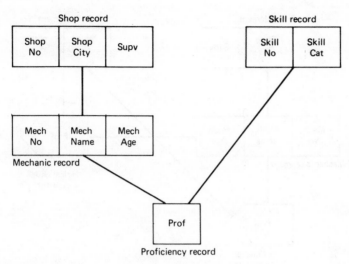

Figure 10.9. Two hierarchies connected to represent the many-to-many relationship.

of just the skill record type. Mechanic and skill, which have a many-to-many relationship to each other, are both in a one-to-many relationship with a specially created record type labeled "proficiency." The skill node, forming the new hierarchy on the right-hand side, is derived from the skill table in Figure 10.7. The proficiency node is derived from the proficiency table in Figure 10.7. Remember that the many-to-many relationship being implemented links mechanic occurrences to skill occurrences. The proficiency table in Figure 10.7 not only indicates those linkages, but gives additional information about them (the proficiency of a particular mechanic in a particular skill).

DL/I. Figure 10.10 shows substantially the same hierarchical structure as shown in Figure 10.9, except that it has been modified to conform to DL/I conventions. The term *record* is replaced by *segment*. The special record type serving as the connector for the many-to-many relationship is called a "logical child" segment. The fact that it appears in both hierarchies (with the proficiency data duplicated in both places in one variation) indicates that the many-to-many relationship can in fact be exercised in both directions. That is, for a given skill, we can find all of the mechanics who have that skill, and, for a given mechanic, we can find all of the skills that he has. If the logical child appeared in only one

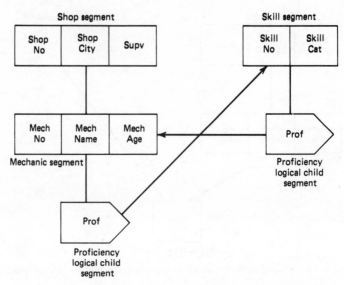

Figure 10.10.   DL/I representation, including a logical relationship.

of the hierarchies, then the relationship could only be traversed from that side.

Access and Performance Modifications.   Substantial work remains after normalization and structuring. The tentative hierarchical structure has to be adjusted for access, performance, and, occasionally, security reasons. This process is sometimes called "physical," as opposed to the earlier "logical," design.

In terms of access, the designer must make an accounting of which fields of which segments must be randomly accessible. The answer will be based on the systems analysis results for the set of applications slated to use the database. Ordinarily, only the root segments can be randomly accessed, and only by their key fields at that (and even the provision of that capability is a decision that has to be made). But suppose that an application requires random access to a field in a nonroot segment. For instance, say that in the current example there is a need to find mechanics randomly by mechanic number. Or, suppose that an application requires random access to a nonkey field in a root segment, for example, a need to find shops randomly by city. Then either secondary indexes must be employed, or the structure must be rearranged so that certain nonroot segments become roots of new hierarchies, with logical relationships employed to connect the new and the old hierarchies together to maintain the appropriate relationships.

Another example of an application-dependent decision is the choice of access methods. Access to the root segments can be either sequential, both indexed and sequential, or random via hashing methods. Such a decision is, of course, based on the needs of the applications that will use the data.

A wide variety of factors must be taken into account in DL/I in terms of performance, many of which are interrelated: A change in one may require a balancing or compensating change in another. For example, long twin chains, for instance, a large number of mechanics working in one shop, can have a deleterious effect on performance because the system does not permit random access into the middle of such a chain. Starting from the beginning of the chain, access can only be made by sequentially traversing the pointer-connected segment occurrences. Depending on the length of the chain, and the number of segment occurrences that can be brought into main memory from disk at one time, traversing such a chain can mean an unacceptable number of time-consuming disk accesses. Among the solutions to this problem are inserting a new, dummy-level segment type above the one with the long twin chains, and, obviously, increasing the number of occurrences that can be read into main memory at one time.

Another example of a performance consideration that should affect the design concerns the number of occurrences of a hierarchy's root segment. Again using the structure in Figure 10.10, assume that there is a fairly small number of shops, but that there are a substantial number of mechanics in each shop. Also assume that most program references will be to mechanic and will presume the knowledge of the mechanic's name or number and shop location. Under these circumstances it makes little sense to have a shop segment root. The capability provided by the IMS access methods of being able to access a root segment randomly, and particularly the speed of such access using the direct organization facility, is extremely powerful and is wasted on a root that has few occurrences. In the case described, the mechanic segment should be made the root, with the shop number field appended to the mechanic number field to form a two-field key. That would create some redundancy in the shop number field, but that kind of key field redundancy has to be considered acceptable under the circumstances. The shop city and supervisor information can be held, still nonredundantly, in a separate, small file.

Other performance considerations, which become more or less important depending on the particular case, include the number of levels (depth) of the hierarchy, the distance from the root of particular segments, relative segment sizes, the use of variable-length segments, and so on.

Data Structuring—Network Databases. The basic principles of database design, using the normalization and structuring approach, are the same in the design of CODASYL network databases as they are in the design of DL/I hierarchies. The set of normalized relations together with a list of the one-to-many and the many-to-many relationships among the entities is the starting point.

Figure 10.11 shows a network constructed from the third normal form relations of Figure 10.7 and the one-to-many relationship (SHOP NO.

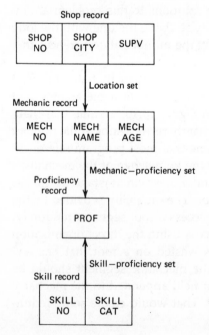

Figure 10.11. CODASYL network representation.

———→≫ MECH NO.) and the many-to-many relationship (MECH NO. ≪——→≫ SKLL NO.) of Figure 10.2. Notice the specification of the 3 "sets" involved. Also notice the "link" record connecting the Mechanic and Skill records which realizes the many-to-many relationship. Just as in the construction of the DL/I database in Figure 10.10, the one-to-many relationship was drawn first, followed by the many-to-many relationship. In the network case, when the time came to draw the many-to-many relationship, the Skill record was added to the network structure that had already been started with the one-to-many relationship between the Shop and the Mechanic records. This procedure stands opposed, technically, to the DL/I case in which a second hierarchy had to be created when the Skill record (or segment) had to be added to the picture.

As for further modifications based on performance issues, the same remarks, in principle, that applied to DL/I, apply here. Factors such as chain lengths, access method types, pointer options, network complexity, and so on, must be considered in the atmosphere of the particular application requirements, the specific DBMS being used, and modifications in the network made on those bases.

Data Structuring—Pseudorelational Databases: Again, in the pseudorelational case, the normalized relations and the one-to-many and many-to-many relationships comprise the jumping-off point for structuring. Structuring consists of basically three steps.

First, a decision has to be made concerning the viability of creating files in the exact form of the normalized relations (since the fundamental data structure in such systems is simple, linear files). There is no question that keeping the files in the same form as the normalized relations is the optimum in terms of minimizing data redundancy. However, in specific instances, the normalization process may produce a large number of relations, each containing a relatively small number of fields. This situation could have an important negative impact on performance and/ or on application programming complexity. In that case it may be necessary to tolerate a certain amount of redundancy in combining the fields from some of the normalized relations to create larger files.

Second, data structures logically linking (actually "joining") various files to each other must be designed. Such structures may take the form of matched, linear lists, as in the ADABAS system, or binary index trees based on concatenated file keys, as in IBM's System/38.

Third, the designer must study the data requirements of the set of applications and determine which fields of each particular file must be accessible on a random basis. Such systems have the ability to have some kind of an index built for each field that has such a requirement.

The Entity-Relationship Model

Introduction. Another major method of database design involves the "entity-relationship model," as described by Peter Chen[2].

Database design using the entity-relationship model begins with a list of the entity types involved and the relationships among them. The philosophy of assuming that the designer knows what the entity types are at the outset is significantly different from the philosophy behind the normalization-based approach. Both methods assume that a thorough systems analysis has been done. But the entity-relationship approach asserts that one of the results of systems analysis is a clear understanding of what the entities involved are. The normalization-based approach takes the view that systems analysis produces a list of the applications' data fields and the relationships among them and that it is then the responsibility of the normalization process to separate the fields that identify entities from those that merely further describe entities, as we have seen.

The entity-relationship approach uses "entity-relationship" diagrams, a hypothetical example of which is shown in Figure 10.12. The rectangular boxes represent entity types, the diamond-shaped box represents a relationship between entities, and the circular figures represent attributes. Thus, Figure 10.12 shows two entities, A and B, which have

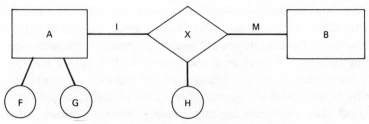

Figure 10.12. The entity-relationship diagram.

a one-to-many relationship X to each other (note the 1 and M on either side of X). Entity A has two attributes (fields describing it) F and G. The relationship X has further descriptive information about it, H. H represents information about the relationship X, that is, about pairs of As and Bs, that does not apply to either an A occurrence by itself or a B occurrence by itself.

Figure 10.13 is an entity-relationship diagram for the fields and relationships shown in Figures 10.1 and 10.2 (the same example used in the normalization-structuring discussion). *Shop, mechanic,* and *skill* have been recognized as the three entities in the application. The one-to-many relationship between shop and mechanic and the many-to-many relationship between mechanic and skill are both clearly displayed. Notice the fields (including the key fields) that describe the entities, and

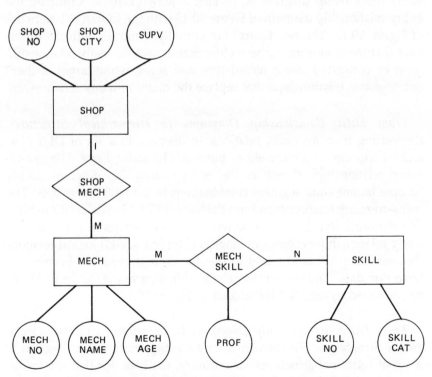

Figure 10.13. Entity-relationship diagram for the sample data.

the proficiency data that further describes the relationship between mechanics and skills.

Other embellishments can be added to entity-relationship diagrams. One such device is a notation to show that occurrences of a particular entity cannot exist in the presence of an occurrence of another entity. Another is an indication that an entity does not have a unique key associated with it and must depend on another entity for proper identification.

From Entity-Relationship Diagrams to CODASYL Network Structures. Finally, the entity-relationship diagram must be converted to a form that corresponds to the data structure of the particular database management system in use. To convert from an entity-relationship diagram to a CODASYL network representation is straightforward: The entity-relationship diagram is, in fact, a network itself. Compare the entity-relationship diagram of Figure 10.13 with the CODASYL network of Figure 10.11. The two figures are virtually identical, with the difference that the connector in the middle of the many-to-many relationship must be converted into a record type and serve as the target of the 2 one-to-many relationships that replace the many-to-many relationship.

From Entity-Relationship Diagrams to Hierarchical Structures. Converting from an entity-relationship diagram to a set of DL/I hierarchies requires a bit more effort, but is still basically direct. The one-to-many relationships shown in the entity-relationship diagram simply become parent-child segment combinations in the DL/I hierarchies. The many-to-many relationships form the basis for DL/I logical relationships. The diamond-shaped box in between the two entities in the many-to-many relationship becomes the logical child in the DL/I logical relationship, and any fields attached to the diamond shaped box become intersection data. Thus the entity-relationship diagram of Figure 10.13 can be converted to the DL/I hierarchies of Figure 10.10.

From Entity-Relationship Diagrams to Relational and Pseudorelational Structures. To convert from an entity-relationship diagram to a set of relational structures, or ordinary, flat files, for that matter, is, in a manner of speaking, a reversal of the design effort using the normalization-based approach. The set of attributes of each entity in the entity-relationship diagram becomes a relation or file, with the unique identifying attribute becoming the key. But, in addition, the identifying attribute of the entity on the "one side" of the one-to-many relationship must be "duplicated" and made one of the attributes of the relation based on the entity on the "many side" of that relationship. Once the network-like diagram is dismantled, this is the only way of keeping track of which occurrence of the entity on the "one" side is related to an occurrence on the "many" side. If there is a multilevel hierarchy of entities, then such duplication must be propagated throughout that hierarchy when converting it to relations or files. In addition, relations or files must be created from the many-to-many relationships found in the entity-relationship diagram. The key of such a relation will consist of the identifying or key fields of the two entities involved, and the nonkey fields will be the relationship modifiers (the fields attached to the diamond-shaped box).

Consider a conversion of the entity-relationship diagram in Figure 10.13 back to the third normal form relations in Figure 10.7. Notice that the shop, mechanic, and skill entities each form the basis for a relation. The mechanic relation must contain a "copy" of the key of the shop

	Normalization Approach	Entity-Relationship Approach
Relational	Normalization	Entity-relationship diagram "dismantled" into a set of relations
Pseudo-relational	Normalization plus join tables or indices	Entity-relationship diagram "dismantled" into a set of relations plus join tables or indices
Hierarchical	Normalization followed by hierarchical structuring	Entity-relationship diagram converted to a hierarchical structure
Network	Normalization followed by network structuring	Entity-relationship diagram converted to a network structure

Figure 10.14. Database design summary chart. (All Results are Subject to Modifications for Performance Reasons.)

relation (SHOP NO.) because it was the target in the one-to-many relationship. The proficiency relation in Figure 10.7 is derived from the
many-to-many relationship between mechanic and skill in Figure 10.13.
Note that the key, MECH NO.–SKLL NO., is formed from the identifying fields of the mechanic and skill entities, and the nonkey field,
"proficiency", was formerly the field connected to the diamond-shaped
relationship connector.

Figure 10.14 is a summary chart of the four DBMS approaches and
the two database design techniques we have discussed.

OTHER TOOLS FOR DATABASE DESIGN

There are several kinds of software tools that can aid in the database
design process.

Automated Database Design Aids

Within the last few years, several automated database design software
products have been introduced. Examples are IBM's Data Base Design
Aid and Database Design Inc.'s Data Designer. Typically, they require
a list of the fields that will comprise the database and the relationships
among those fields. In general they are capable of performing logical
database design, and, in some cases with partial human intervention,
physical database design for specific database management systems. As
part of their operation they can perform editing on the input data and
in so doing find errors and inconsistencies.

Database design programs have met with mixed success in the field.
The biggest complaint from their users is that specifying the fields and
relationships in the depth and precision required (of any computer program) is too time consuming. That, however, is an unfortunate attitude
since the set of fields and relationships *must* be specified precisely for
database design, whether or not an automated tool is to be used. The
result of doing otherwise is inevitably a poor database design.

Performance Prediction and Monitoring Aids

Once the logical and physical database designs are complete, there are
various methodologies available to predict the eventual performance of

the system. In order to be accurate enough to be of any real use, these methodologies must consider a substantial amount of information beyond the structure of the database. For example, they must also consider the relative frequency of occurrence of the different record types, the application program calling patterns, and the resource competition from other applications using the same or different databases. Some of the methodologies have been partially automated as simulation routines.

CONCLUSION

Once the database design process is completed, the focus of the application development process turns to the programmers. Presumably, program design was taking place simultaneously with database design. Thus the programmers can at once be presented with their coding assignments, and with the necessary data structures to use.

Beyond coding are the remaining steps in the sequence. These include various levels of program testing, installation, and ongoing maintenance. All of the steps from programming through maintenance will be greatly benefited by the careful and continuously flowing work that was done from the earliest stages of the application development process through database design.

REFERENCES

1. Chen, P. P., and Yao, S. B., "Design and Performance Tools for Data Base Systems," *Proceedings of the Third International Conference on Very Large Data Bases*, Tokyo, October 6–8, 1977, pp. 3–15.
2. Chen, P. P. S., "Applications of the Entity-Relationship Model," *Proceedings of the NYU Symposium on Database Design*, New York, May 18–19, 1978, pp. 25–33.

BIBLIOGRAPHY

Curtice, R. M., "Data Base Design Using a CODASYL System," *Proceedings of the ACM Annual Conference*, San Diego, November 1974, pp. 473–480.

Curtice, R. M., and Jones, P. E., *Logical Data Base Design*, Van Nostrand Reinhold, New York, 1982.

Date, C. J., *An Introduction to Database Systems*, 3d ed., Addison-Wesley, Reading, MA, 1981.

Gerritsen, R., "A Preliminary System for the Design of DBTG Data Structures," *Communications of the ACM*, vol. 18, no. 10, October 1975, pp. 551–557

Hubbard, G. U., *Computer-Assisted Data Base Design*, Van Nostrand Reinhold, New York, 1981.

Inmon, W. H., *Effective Data Base Design*, Prentice-Hall, Englewood Cliffs, NJ, 1981.

Navathe, S. B., and Schkolnick, M., "View Representation in Logical Database Design," *Proceedings of the SIGMOD International Conference on Management of Data*, Austin, TX, May 31 and June 1–2, 1978, pp. 144–156.

Ng, P. A., "Further Analysis of the Entity-Relationship Approach to Database Design," *IEEE Transactions on Software Engineering*, vol. SE-7, no. 1, January 1981, pp. 85–99.

Novak, D. O., and Fry, J. P., "The State of the Art of Logical Database Design," *Proceedings of the Fifth Texas Conference on Computing Systems*, Austin, TX, October 18–19, 1976, pp. 30–38.

Perron, R., *Design Guide for CODASYL Data Base Management Systems*, Q.E.D. Information Sciences, Wellesley, MA, 1981.

Teorey, T. J., and Fry, J. P., "The Logical Record Access Approach to Database Design," *Computing Surveys*, vol. 12, no. 2, June, 1980, pp. 179–211.

Teorey, T. J., and Fry, J. P., *Design of Database Structures*, Prentice-Hall, Englewood Cliffs, NJ, 1982.

Vetter, M., and Maddison, R. N., *Database Design Methodology*, Prentice-Hall, Englewood Cliffs, NJ, 1981.

QUESTIONS FOR THOUGHT

1. Describe the reasons for the importance of good database design. How can a poor physical design weaken a good logical design? Can a good physical design make up for the weaknesses of a poor logical design?

2. Consider the data normalization process. What is required as input to it? What does the process accomplish? Do you think that the process can be automated? What is its value if the intended database structure is hierarchical or network in nature?

3. Is it more desirable for a database designer to be an expert in the technical details of the database design process, or in the way that the business function, being automated in the application, works? How does that relate to the background of the systems analyst working on the same application development project? What if one and the same person does both the systems analysis and database design work on an application?

The Process Integrated

11

Methodology Interfaces

DATA: THE ESSENCE OF BUSINESS ORGANIZATION

Organization Types

Organizations can be classified into a wide variety of types, such as manufacturing companies, retailers, transportation companies, banks, universities, government bodies, and so on. Every organization, regardless of which category it falls into, has data to manage.

We have seen that data can be discussed in terms of data classes in the strategic planning systems, and in terms of fields at the systems analysis level. Data can also be discussed according to the type of business organization in which it is found: the data-intensive organization versus the non-data-intensive organization.

Data in Data-Intensive Organizations

Certain organizations, by the nature of their business or reason for being, are data-intensive. Among the purest examples of these organizations are financial institutions: banks, insurance companies, stock brokers, and so forth. Such firms manage data as their primary resource, in the sense of money, loans, insurance claims, and stock buy or sell orders, to name only a few. One could argue that there really are physical entities involved—dollar bills, insurance claim forms, stock certificates— but they are meaningless apart from the data they represent. One could also argue, quite correctly, that such firms do have physical items to manage, such as people, offices, and computers, but these are all accessories that aid in the management of the primary commodity: data.

Such organizations must plan very carefully how they run their operations. The data is the crucial thing, without which there is no business. These firms have been heavy data processing equipment users since the advent of the computer and have recognized that to stay competitive, they must continually be at the state-of-the-art of data processing.

In data-intensive organizations, business strategic planning has always, because of the nature of the business, focused on data. Clearly, an astute management will use such planning in its information systems strategic planning. The natural flow should then continue into detailed systems analysis and database design, as previously described.

Data in Non-Data-Intensive Organizations

The physical resources that non-data intensive organizations produce or are otherwise involved with are mirrored by data. Thus an automobile moving down an assembly line, as well as the people working on it, its eventual buyer, and the assembly line itself, are all represented by some kind of data in a computer.

Here, although not the organization's product, the data is a crucial resource, nonetheless. Data may not be involved in a firm's business strategic planning, but is as essential a part of the information systems strategic planning phase as for data-intensive firms.

DATA: THE COMMON ELEMENT

Whichever of the two data orientations an organization has, the common element is data. Data is a corporate resource, and successful data processing requires careful planning and a smooth flow of thought concerning data. We have spoken of four major phases of corporate operations which, when linked in a chain, form the four steps in the consideration of data. Of great concern, then, are the interfaces between those phases.

Interface Between Business Strategic Planning and Information Systems Strategic Planning

The interface between the business strategic planning and information systems strategic planning stages is critically important and growing more so. It is also the least well defined of the three stages that we have been discussing.

In the early days of data processing, individual applications were selected for automation without regard to related applications. Gradually, planning for the data processing requirements of several related applications was begun but remained at a relatively low level. Now, with the increasingly massive degree to which computers have permeated today's organizations, planning for a firm's information processing requirements must take place at the very highest levels.

At the point that an organization sets its business objectives for the next plan period, it decides the levels of the various resources that it can commit. Modern organizations must include information processing as one of those resources. As a firm moves from thinking about its business objectives to strategic information resource planning, it must be clear, on a broad level, how much capital it is willing to commit to computer hardware, data processing personnel, floor space for both, and so on. To do less at this stage in the development of computer usage would be to leave the data processing organization obliged to provide computer support in an impromptu fashion. The results, in that case, cannot be as beneficial as they might be.

Interface between Information Systems Strategic Planning and Detailed Systems Analysis

The interface between information systems strategic planning and systems analysis, though elusive, must not be ignored.

A basic premise, when entering the systems analysis phase of application development, is that the goals and bounds of the application be understood. Unfortunately, all too often, this is not the case, and even when it is, the application stands independently of related applications. This situation can and must be remedied by following a careful flow from the information systems strategic planning phase.

The result of the strategic plan is a broad, interconnected outline of the organization's information resource requirements. Portions of that plan can be carved out for detailed analysis and implementation as individual applications. The clear and compelling advantage of this procedure is that after development, each application system can be related back to the overall information systems plan. Data processing management can keep track of the interfaces between the various applications, understanding how a change in one will affect others. Rather than existing as independent entities, each application becomes part of the overall information-processing network of the organization. At the same time, the data needs of an individual application can be satisfied on a shared basis with those of others.

Interface between Detailed Systems Analysis and Database Design

Of the three interfaces, the one between detailed systems analysis and database design has the longest history of practical use. This is not meant to imply, however, that its use in many installations has been sufficient.

It is clear that before reaching the database design stage (and the program design stage), a full and clear understanding of the manner of operation of the business process being automated must be gained. Specifically, the database designers must be provided with a list of the data fields involved in the application and with a list of the operative relationships between those fields.

Since the essence of detailed systems analysis *is* understanding and documenting the business process, and since part of the output from it are the lists of fields and relationships, the interface between the two phases is quite direct.

DATA: THE CONTINUOUS FLOW

The interfaces between the two levels of strategic planning, systems analysis, and database design are clear and apparent. There was a time in data processing history when data processing managers thought of those four processes as independent and only marginally related. Business strategic planners seemed to ignore data processing, and the gaps between the other three processes seemed to be wide. Beginning each process appeared to be an exercise in starting from scratch.

In fact there *is* a continuous flow of thought and activity from business strategic planning to database design. With data as the link, the processes flow from one to the next in an organized fashion. That recognition is a modern step in making the field of data processing a more mature, organized, manageable, and, ultimately, successful discipline.

QUESTIONS FOR THOUGHT

1. Describe the advantages of the "continuous flow approach".
2. What is the nature of the data passed from:
   a. Business strategic planning to information systems strategic planning?
   b. Information systems strategic planning to detailed systems analysis?
   c. Detailed systems analysis to database design?

3. What problems might arise if a poor interface exists between:
   a. Business strategic planning and information systems strategic planning?
   b. Information systems strategic planning and detailed systems analysis?
   c. Detailed systems analysis and database design?
4. Is there a parallel between the four phases of information planning and design that we have discussed in this book, and phases of planning and design in other areas of the business organization, such as finance, manufacturing, etc.?
5. Are there any other major steps that should be interwoven among or at the ends of the four phases that we have discussed here?

12

The Future

DATA: A CORPORATE RESOURCE

We have established data as a valuable corporate asset. Data mirrors the workings of an organization and provides a unique insight into the way that it functions.

We are inexorably moving toward an information-oriented society in which organizations will have tremendous information demands placed on them, both from within and from without. The internal demands will come from all levels of the organization. In the future there will be few operational aspects that will not be "computerized." But in addition, there will be a much stronger emphasis on information demands coming from middle and upper management, as a means of aiding decision making. The external information demands will come from virtually all of the types of entities with which the organization interfaces: suppliers, creditors, customers, governments agencies, and so forth.

All manner of data, in addition to the standard accounting-related data, will take on much more value. There will be increasingly sophisticated uses for data about competitors, manufacturing processes, markets, and product design, and an endless array of data about all aspects of the organization's workings. Furthermore, the interdisciplinary use of data, such as feeding design data into manufacturing processes, will have an important effect on fundamental changes in the functioning of an organization. Such data uses will be correctly perceived as providing a true competitive advantage in the firm's marketplace.

INFORMATION RESOURCE MANAGEMENT

Data Administration Today

We have made the point that a manageable resource requires a group of people to manage it. Today, such groups to manage data exist in an embryonic form in most large organizations. Most of them are concerned entirely or primarily with the data related to the database management system. Such data administration groups are, as we have seen, usually divided into two subgroups: one to manage the data on an operational basis, and another to plan and design for the data environment.

Managing Data in the Future

In the future, data administration will encompass far greater volumes of data than it does today for at least three reasons. One, rather obviously, will be the increased amount of data in existence because of the expanded emphasis on data processing. Another is the fact that an increasing percentage of data processing is being done with database management systems technology. The third is that data administration organizations will take on responsibility for a larger proportion of data in files not under the control of the database management system.

As the level of strategic planning increases, the degree to which data is shared among different departments will also increase. Data will be thought of as a shareable resource to be used to advantage, not as the private possession of a particular department for a particular application. As that attitude about data grows, so will the size and range of abilities of the internal organization whose charter it is to manage a firm's data. The proportion of data administration personnel relative to the set of programmers and systems analysts will increase, as the former assumes more of the data-related tasks in the shared environment.

But, even more, there will be a world of data management beyond data administration: information resource management (IRM). In addition to the data-files-oriented scope of data administration, information resource management will encompass the management of other forms of data. For example, as data processing and word processing systems become more highly integrated, the data in the word processing systems will come under IRM control. As computer graphics develops, much of the organization's pictorial data will be managed by IRM. As programmable robots come into greater use, IRM will be involved with a variety of manufacturing data which today's data processing departments do not know.

We do not wish to imply that IRM is necessarily an offshoot of data processing and that computer professionals will inherit the mantle of IRM managers. IRM is an integrating term for all of the audio, pictorial, word, and data-coded items that an organization requires to become efficient. Managers of secretaries, word processing specialists, communications specialists, librarians, records retention personnel, and even employees concerned with standards, are all currently working in areas to which IRM is related. IRM is an evolutionary task that integrates the information of an organization.

THE UBIQUITOUS COMPUTER

The stage of information resource management will be set by the proliferation of computer and communications equipment. In addition to more powerful large processors, the number and uses of small processors will accelerate. Virtually all typewriters will become word processors, tied into larger information systems. Computer graphics equipment and programmable manufacturing devices will grow in use. Voice, text, and other data will become highly accessible and readily transferable to all parts of the organization through massive communications networks. Interfaces between man and machine will become increasingly more natural, allowing totally untrained personnel to take greater advantage of the information resource.

The result of all of this hardware, coupled with the information resource management concept, will be that virtually everyone in an organization will have access to tremendous amounts of information. It is impossible to predict all of the ramifications of such an environment.

THE THOROUGHLY PLANNED ENVIRONMENT

Future corporate executives will rely on accumulated information for decision making much more so than their counterparts do today. That is not to say that they will cease relying on intuition gained by experience, but rather that they will have far more of an information base to make informed decisions with. Even those inclined to do otherwise will find themselves using their information resources to stay competitive with competing firms whose executives are using such data.

Part of the emphasis on an informed management style will be increasingly sophisticated planning. Planning, both in terms of business objectives and in terms of information resources is, as we have suggested here, the intelligent way to guide an organization over a period of time. The essence of planning is data: production data, sales history, manpower levels, and so on.

The relationship which we have described between business strategic planning and information systems strategic planning will continue to gain in importance. The carefully prepared business plan of the future will be useless without a carefully planned information system to support it. Planning for the information system must be included in the overall business planning cycle.

THE THOROUGHLY ANALYZED ENVIRONMENT

In the new information age, there will be less room for undocumented, informal work procedures above a certain level of detail. Each business process must be thoroughly analyzed and understood, for several reasons. One is the issue of management control. A sophisticated manager should now, and must in the future, be aware of all that is taking place beneath him in order to exercise a proper level of control. Another reason is interchangeability of personnel. And a third reason is that in order to make the entire operation run as smoothly as possible, each of its components must be understood. With that understanding, modifications can be made to individual processes to make their interaction with other processes more efficient.

The systems analyst will thus become the new industrial engineer of the information age. He will be equipped with tools that he can apply across all of the aspects of the organization to understand, document, and, when necessary, modify the business procedures. Using common techniques, he will be at the forefront of converting the strategic plans into practice. Middle and upper management will call upon him as a consultant when they have to delve into specific operational procedures.

THE CAREFULLY PLANNED AND SHARED DATABASE

The benefits of the database approach to data management have already become apparent to most organizations today. The reduced data redundancy, improved data independence, heightened data integration, and enhanced data consistency that the approach achieves are improving the efficiency of all types of firms. The future will see the database approach used to such a degree that the only data files not controlled by the database management system will be special-purpose or temporary local files in locally supported equipment.

The increasingly widespread use of database management systems, the growth of information resource management as a managerial style, and the increased use of data that we have described will change the emphasis surrounding data and data processing. The data will be seen to be the critical asset of the organization, whereas the means of accessing that data, the "data processing," will appear to be a secondary, mechanical feature. Put simply, the emphasis in the term "data processing" has always been on the *processing*. In the future it will be on the *data*.

CONCLUSION

Data is the key to the management of organizations in the future. Through careful planning, thoroughly analyzed business procedures, and a well-organized store of data, the corporate manager of the future will be able to exercise control in an informed, intelligent manner. It will truly be a major step in moving from the industrial age to the information age.

BIBLIOGRAPHY

Dertouzos, M. L., and Moses, J., eds., *The Computer Age: A Twenty-Year View*, MIT Press, Cambridge, MA, 1979.

Synnott, W. R., and Gruber, W. H., *Information Resource Management*, Wiley, New York, 1981.

QUESTIONS FOR THOUGHTS

1. Several trends seem to be emerging in data processing. They include an emphasis on distributed processing, office automation, personal computers, and the information center concept. Based on those trends, consider the data processing environment ten years from now and postulate what the nature of the data administration organization will be. Include its duties, organization, interfaces with

other data processing departments, and placement in the corporate organization.

2. With the increasing emphasis that is being placed on planning and systems analysis, speculate on:

   a. The growth of personnel in such functions in the future.

   b. The backgrounds of the personnel in such functions in the future.

   c. The placement in the corporate organization of such functions in the future.

   d. The influence on the corporation of such functions in the future.

Index